THE
Hero of Faithfulness

God's Attributes on Display in Hebrews 11

Steve Barckholtz

Copyright © 2013 by Steve Barckholtz

THE Hero of Faithfulness
God's Attributes on Display in Hebrews 11
by Steve Barckholtz

Printed in the United States of America

ISBN 9781625098832

All rights reserved solely by the author. The author guarantees all contents are original and do not infringe upon the legal rights of any other person or work. No part of this book may be reproduced in any form without the permission of the author. The views expressed in this book are not necessarily those of the publisher.

Unless otherwise indicated, Bible quotations are taken from *THE MESSAGE* version of the Bible. Copyright © 1993, 1994, 1995, 1996, 2000, 2001, 2002 by NavPress Publishing Group. Used by permission; The Holy Bible, *New International Version®, NIV®*. Copyright © 1973, 1978, 1984, 2011 by Biblica, Inc.™ Used by permission of Zondervan. www.zondervan.com; The New King James Version® (NKJV). Copyright © 1982 by Thomas Nelson, Inc. Used by permission; The Holy Bible, English Standard Version® (ESV®). Copyright © 2001 by Crossway, a publishing ministry of Good News Publishers. Used by permission; The NEW AMERICAN STANDARD BIBLE® (NASB). Copyright © 1960, 1962, 1963, 1968, 1971, 1972, 1973, 1975, 1977, 1995 by The Lockman Foundation; The Holy Bible, New Living Translation (NLT). Copyright © 1996, 2004, 2007 by Tyndale House Foundation. Used by permission of Tyndale House Publishers, Inc., Carol Stream, Illinois 60188; The Amplified® Bible (AMP). Copyright © 1954, 1958, 1962, 1964, 1965, 1987 by The Lockman Foundation Used by permission; and The King James Bible.

www.xulonpress.com

Contents

Introduction- God: THE Hero of Faithfulness (11:1-2)..................ix

  1. Creation: God's Nature (11:3) 15
  2. Abel: God's Absence (11:4) 22
  3. Enoch: God's Pleasure (11:5-6)...30
  4. Noah: God's Intimacy (11:7) 39
  5. Abram: God's Call (11:8-10) 47
  6. Sarah: God's Joy (11:11-12) 56

Interlude- God's Sovereignty (11:13-16)...66

  7. Abraham & Isaac: God's Intervention (11:17-19)...................73
  8. Isaac: God's Heritage (11:20) 81
  9. Jacob: God's Blessings (11:21) 91
10. Joseph: God's Dreams (11:22) 100
11. Moses' Parents: God's Beauty (11:23) 109
12. Moses: God's Development (11:24-28).....................................118
13. Israel & The Red Sea: God's Glory (11:29) 128
14. Israel & Jericho: God's Posture (11:30) 137
15. Rahab: God's Inclusivity (11:31)..146

Interlude- God's Sovereignty. . . Continues (11:32) 155

16. Gideon: God's Vulnerability (11:32-38) 163
17. Barak: God's Position (11:32-38)..173
18. Samson: God's Strength (11:32-38) 182

19. Jephthah: God's Promise (11:32-38)..........................190
20. David: God's Heart (11:32-38) 198
21. Samuel: God's Ear (11:32-38) 207
22. The Prophets: God's Focus (11:32-38) 215
23. Us: God's Plan (11:39-40)..224

Conclusion- God: THE Hero of Faithfulness (Hebrews 12:1-3)....233
Endnotes 239
Acknowledgements..245

For Wendy
You are my hero
Thank you for your
FAITHFULNESS
To God
To Zane & Mallory
To me

Introduction

"God: The Hero of Faithfulness"

One afternoon, as I was sitting in my office writing a sermon, I was listening to Pandora Radio on the computer. All of a sudden, time stopped. A song I never remembered hearing grabbed my soul—

I am broken, I am bleeding
I am scared and I'm confused
But You are faithful
Yes, You are faithful...

...When I cannot have the answers that I'm wanting to demand
I'll remember You are God and everything is in Your hands
With Your hands you put the sun and moon, the stars up in the sky
For the sake of love, You hung your own Son on the cross to die

When You give, when You take away
Even then, great is Your faithfulness
Great is Your faithfulness
And with everything inside of me
I am choosing to believe
You are faithful...[1]

The song, fittingly and simply entitled *Faithful*, was written by Steven Curtis Chapman following the tragic death of his daughter. While I cannot—thank You, Jesus!—know the degree of brokenness and confusion such a horror brings, the day I first heard this song, I was scared and confused. That day my faith felt so weak, I almost felt faith-less.

As those words washed over me and resonated through me, it seemed God's faithfulness was just about the only thing I had left. But what a "thing"!

First and foremost, in absolutely everything, God is faithful to Himself and to His promises and purposes and Person!

In addition (and without fail!), God is also always faithful to us—His beloved children!

> From His "give and take" nature, God is faithful!
> No matter the day. . . or the circumstance. . . God is faithful!
> Regardless of the situation. . . or the generation. . . God is faithful!

Given this unconditional faithfulness of Almighty God, in I Corinthians 15, Paul bluntly reminds us—"If only for this life we have hope in Christ, we are to be pitied more than all men. But Christ has indeed been raised from the dead, the firstfruits of those who have fallen asleep" (I Corinthians 15:19-20, NIV).

In Hebrews 10, the challenge to living out our faith takes this shape—

> "So let's do it—full of belief, confident that we're presentable inside and out. Let's keep a firm grip on the promises that keep us going. [God] always keeps His word. Let's see how inventive we can be in encouraging love and helping out, not avoiding worshiping together as some do but spurring each other on, especially as we see the big Day approaching" (Hebrews 10:22-25).

This passage from Hebrews 10, especially as Eugene Peterson renders it in *The Message*, contains two words and images that jump to the foreground. First, is this challenge—"Let's see how INVENTIVE we can be. . ."

Thomas Edison famously said—"I have not failed. I have just found 10,000 ways that do not work."[2] Too often, the Christian Church is too afraid to try anything new or different for fear of failure. Too frequently, inventiveness is frowned upon in the Church. Not only that, creative thinking and expansive imagination are sometimes seen as heretical.

Instead of a culture of inventiveness, "church" has been reduced to a culture of status quo. Too frequently, "church" is a place in which everyone already has all the answers to all the questions—even if they are answers to questions no one is asking anymore (if they ever were asking them in the first place!).

The second image from Hebrews 10 that Eugene Peterson brings out is in the phrase—"spurring each other on. . ." For several years in the mid-1990s, Wendy and I took our vacation in late October and early November to help her family with the fall cattle round-up. Each day, long before the sun came up, we would leave the family farm in southern Idaho. We would head down Highway 93 to the San Jacinto Ranch, south of Jackpot, Nevada. After a quick breakfast, we would saddle our horses and trailer them out to whichever rangeland or pasture we would be gathering cows and calves from that day.

As something more than a novice, but (far!) less than an expert, I had two simple goals each day—stay on the horse and stay out of the real cowboys' way.

I looked the part—with a big, black, Resistol cowboy hat and down-at-the-heels boots. One year, I even sported a finely waxed handle-bar moustache. Inside my Wranglers, however, I knew I wasn't a real cowboy. I could talk the talk. I could strike the pose, scuff the dirt, and amble along with a convincing bow-legged shuffle. But in reality, I was a preacher on vacation. I was a guy enjoying the scenery, relaxing while working. And just in case I started thinking I really was a cowboy, there was one more reason I knew I was really a city slicker on horseback—I never got to wear spurs.

Spurs were worn by the real cowboys. Spurs were worn by the people who knew how to use them. Spurs were worn by the men and women who knew the proper technique and touch for putting the rowels to the horse's flesh. A wanna-be buckaroo like me would just kick the horse and cause panic and trouble. A real cowboy knew how to touch and when to spur for the purpose of getting horse and cattle to accomplish a specific task.

Here's the bottom-line—spurs hurt! Spurs cause pain! Yet Hebrews 10 tells us from the midst of inventively encouraging, loving, and helping each other, we are also to "spur each other on." In other words, the relationships we have with each other in the church might involve some kicking and some pain—but this pain is always to be for a purpose.

When a real cowboy spurs his horse, it brings some purposeful pain to the horse, but the use of spurs also leads to the efficient gathering of cattle. Our spurring and encouraging each other in the church is for the purpose of inventively and creatively and energetically presenting God's faithfulness to the world. We are to "spur each other on" as we present God's grace and blessing through Jesus Christ to the people around us.

Here, then, is the ultimate question to wrestle with throughout these pages—

- Are you ready to leave behind a "status quo faith" and, instead, put your faith into risk-filled action?

Hebrews 11:1-2 says—"Now faith is the assurance of things hoped for, the conviction of things not seen. For by it the people of old received their commendation" (Hebrews 11:1-2, ESV). The "assurance" and "conviction" of the English Standard Version is rendered by Eugene Peterson in *The Message*, as "the fundamental fact." Sometimes we are so quick to talk about faith that we forget "the fundamental fact" of faith is that it requires an object.

From Abel and Enoch, to David, Samuel, and the prophets, the object of the faith of the men and women in Hebrews 11 was the same—THE Hero. The object of these ancients' faith was "THE Hero of Faithfulness"—the Triune God, Father, Son, and Holy Spirit.

Each man and woman in Hebrews 11 was remarkably like me that lonely, scary, confusing day in my office. Every person and situation in Hebrews 11 reveals the same struggles you and I deal with in our daily lives. Like the ancients of Hebrews 11, you and I live with a faith that is weak yet strong, and before we know it, weak again. We are faithful then faith-less, then faithful and faith-less all over again. This weak/

strong, faithful/faith-less cycle is more agitating and turbulent than the super heavy wash cycle of a wash machine!

As we journey from creation to the cross, we will see over and over again the clear truth of Hebrews 11:1&2—

> The fundamental fact of existence is that this trust in God, this faith, is the firm foundation under everything that makes life worth living. [This faith is] our handle on what we can't see. The act of faith is what distinguished our ancestors, set them above the crowd (Hebrews 11:1&2).

As we study each life listed in Hebrews 11, we will find the most "fundamental fact of [all] existence"—God, "The Hero of Faithfulness," is absolutely consistent and unflinchingly faithful to Himself and to all of His creation.

Not only was "The Hero of Faithfulness" consistent and faithful to those ancient patriarchs, God is also absolutely consistent and unflinchingly faithful to us. Not only did "The Hero of Faithfulness" set them apart, He wants to set us apart today. "The Hero of Faithfulness" wants you and me to be shining examples to the world around us! "The Hero of Faithfulness" is calling and leading us to live out our faith inventive and creative ways today!

Let's put our spurs on and ride through the lives of these ancient men and women. Along the way, as we see how faithful God was to them, we will learn how faithful He still is to us!

Chapter 1

"Creation: God's Nature"

It was one of those March days that defies category. Was it late winter, or early spring? The sun was bright. The clouds were high. The wind was almost nonexistent. The temperature had climbed all the way to the upper 40s.

While Wendy and Mallory made craft projects and watched puppet shows in the Visitor Center, Zane and I went on a ranger-led snowshoe hike at the Sawtooth National Recreation Area, north of Ketchum, Idaho.

Listening to our snowshoes crunch as we followed the ranger across the snow, our first stop was before an impressive beaver lodge. The lodge above ground was still covered in snow, but the pond below was no longer frozen over. Unfortunately, no beaver were to be seen.

Undaunted, we continued making our way along the trail, until we stopped to study the layers in the snow. While Zane and I caught our breath, the ranger gave us a quick lesson in avalanche patterns and causes.

As our journey continued across an open meadow, the ranger suddenly stopped us next to a small stand of aspen trees. With hardly contained excitement, the ranger yanked off her gloves and rubbed the tree trunk. Then she showed us her hand. A gray-white substance covered her skin. "Any guesses what this is?" she asked.

Zane shrugged, having no idea.

Feeling fairly cocky and overly sure of myself, I offered, "Pollen?"

"Good guess, but no."

The explanation that followed was stunning. Following forest fires, quakies are among the first trees to regrow in the denuded area. Because of their "First-to-the-Frontier" nature, aspens are exposed for great lengths of time to the full intensity of the sun. As time goes by, other trees slowly grow alongside the quakies. Finally, after several years, the aspens have a source of shade. During these lonely times of renewal following a forest fire, the aspens produce a dust-like substance that is, essentially, sunscreen to protect their bark from the harsh, burning effects of the sun.

For the rest of our snowshoe hike, I was transfixed by thoughts about the nature of God.

- What kind of God cares so deeply about a silly old aspen tree that He calls it into existence with its own SPF compound. . . that doesn't even smell like Hawaiian Tropic!

As Hebrews 11 enters its recitation of God's faithfulness to various men and women of the Old Testament, the starting point in the litany is creation—"By faith, we see the world called into existence by God's word, what we see created by what we don't see" (Hebrews 11:3).

Stop and think about that phrase—

- "We see the world called into existence by God's word."

Think about the nature of the God who called this world into existence. Think about the power of the God who created this world when nothing—NOTHING!—existed before. Think about the God who created this world we can see and experience.

What does it tell us about God's nature that He created a specific species of tree—*Populus tremula*—and He created it so intimately and carefully that is comes with its own sunscreen?

It might be tempting to respond coarsely and quickly that God loves us more than some old, gnarly, bunch of Basque-engraved aspen trees. But our human selfishness misses the point concerning God's nature.

The fact that God's love for His chief creation—humankind—is unparalleled should be a given. What we need to also recognize is that

"Creation: God's Nature"

loving us in such depth and detail does not come at the expense of creating, knowing, and caring for the intricate properties of any of His other creations.

Even though we know Galileo proved the sun was at the center of the universe, we still are pretty quick to place ourselves at the center of everything. We are tempted to think God loves us so much He probably doesn't have that much love left over for other things—like a bunch of silly quakies along a lonely streambed.

WRONG!

God's love for us numbers the hairs on our heads. God's love for us tracks the miles of vessels in our circulatory system. God's love for us knows every one of the cells of our skin—including the ones that just silently fell off while you read this page.

The nature of God and the breadth of His love is also such that He creates absolutely everything with the same attention to intimacy and detail and uniqueness.

Stop and take a break from your reading. Go on a hike. Sit in the city park. Tour your neighborhood. Get outside and look around—

- That squirrel flitting along the fence line—intimately known by God.
- Those lenticular wave clouds crossing the sky—majestically drawn by God's hand.
- The yellow lab lying in the neighbor's driveway—crafted and created by God's design.

As you look around and take in all the creations God has called into existence, recognize each one as the gift and blessing it is. For that matter, try to keep track of and count all God's blessings. For one hour, count every single blessing and gift from God that you can see, smell, taste, hear, recall, remember, touch, or encounter. At the end of an hour, what tally of blessings did you get?

- Multiply your total by 70 times 7
- Multiply that number by 10,000 times 10,000

What total do you have now? A pretty impressive number, I'm sure! Guess what? That is still only a mere fraction of the blessings God actually showered around you in that hour!

Given all this grace and blessing and generosity of God's, here is our perpetual challenge—how do we NOT lose track of the generosity and grace of the Hero of Faithfulness amidst the abundance of His blessings?

Paul's doxology in Romans 11 helps keep us focused on our Hero—

> Oh, the depth of the riches of the wisdom and knowledge of God! How unsearchable His judgments, and His paths beyond tracing out! 'Who has known the mind of the Lord? Or who has been His counselor?' 'Who has ever given to God, that God should repay him?' For from Him and through Him and to Him are all things. To Him be the glory forever! Amen (Romans 11:33-36, NIV).

In March 2012, movie-maker and adventurer James Cameron journeyed to the bottom of the Mariana Trench in a one-man submersible.

Before I even continue with James Cameron's story, stop and think about the Mariana Trench.

Did you count the Mariana Trench in your list of blessings and gifts from God's generous nature? What about the creatures living at the bottom of the Mariana Trench? What does the very existence of shrimp-like arthropods seven miles below the Pacific Ocean's surface tell us about the nature of God?

An inhabited environment, in a canyon almost 1600 miles long, with an average width of 40 miles, located almost 7 miles beneath the surface of the Pacific Ocean. The Mariana Trench dwarfs the Grand Canyon. What was God thinking?

For the majority of history, since God called it into existence, the very existence of the Mariana Trench has been unknown. Except, God knew He had placed it where it is. And, God knew every species and organism living there. And, God made each creature found only in those dark waters, with such intimacy and care that it is able to withstand the extreme pressure and darkness and cold and isolation of such deep, deep waters.

In interviews following his historic journey, James Cameron said, "When I got to the bottom. . . it was completely featureless and uniform. . . . My feeling was one of complete isolation from all of humanity. . . . More than anything, (it's) realizing how tiny you are down in this big, vast, black, unknown and unexplored place."[1]

Here is what James Cameron, as well as each of us need to recognize—God knew from before He created time that in the spring of 2012AD, James Cameron would descend into "this big vast, black, unknown and unexplored place." Therein lies another bit of God's nature revealed for us. Nothing surprises God.

The existence of tiny shrimp-like arthropods seven miles beneath the ocean's surface might surprise us—not God. He called each and every single one of them into existence by His Word. The sovereign God of the universe places each of His creations precisely where and when He wants it to be.

The technology needed to create a one-man submersible capable of descending to the depths of the ocean (and of returning safely back to the surface!) might amaze us—not God. He called the "laws" of nature and physics into existence by His Word. He created the metals necessary to manufacture the hull of *Deep Sea Challenger*. He provided the wisdom to power the computers of the submersible.

For us, there is great comfort to be found in knowing the nature of God is such that He knows all and is surprised by nothing.

One of the most revealing scenes of God's sovereign nature and His intimate creative abilities in all of Scripture is recorded in the last chapters of Job.

Following all Job's suffering, and after all his friends' clichéd answers, finally when their mighty protestations were completed, God speaks to Job. Job 38:1 says—"Now, finally, God answered Job from the eye of a violent storm. He said. . ." (Job 38:1).

What follows from the quiet center of this mighty storm is about 70 verses of God thundering at least 39 exceedingly specific questions at Job—

- Where were you when I created the earth?
- Who decided on its size?
- How was its foundation poured?

- Have you ever gotten to the true bottom of things, explored the labyrinthine caves of deep ocean?
- Have you ever traveled to where snow is made?
- Do you know the month when mountain goats give birth?
- Who do you think set the wild donkey free?
- Was it through your know-how that the hawk learned to fly, soaring effortlessly on thermal updrafts?

Finally, God takes a breath and waits for a response. From the eye of the storm, God looks Job in the eye—"Now what do you have to say for yourself? Are you going to haul Me, the Mighty One, into court and press charges?" (Job 40:1-2).

Give Job credit.

When we are confronted with our issues, we, usually, keep on babbling nonsense. We dig our holes deeper. We quickly (and repeatedly!) forget the first step in getting out of a hole is to stop digging.

Give Job credit. He stops digging. Job responds to God's litany, saying—"I'm speechless, in awe—words fail me. I should never have opened my mouth! I've talked too much, way too much. I'm ready to shut up and listen" (Job 40:3-5).

Job 40&41, then, unfold another 17 or so more questions from God to Job—

- Look at Behemoth, I created him as well as you.
- Can you pull in the sea beast, Leviathan, with a fly rod and stuff him in your creel?

The cymbal-crash of ultimate revelation comes from the eye of the storm in Job 41:11 as God reveals one of the greatest attributes of His nature—"I'm in charge of all this—I run this universe!" (Job 41:11).

In the presence of the God who is in charge of all creation because He called all created things into existence by His Word, will we be sensible enough to join Job—

I'm convinced: You can do anything and everything. Nothing and no one can upset Your plans. You asked, 'Who is this muddying the water, ignorantly confusing the issue, second-guessing My purposes?' I admit it. I was the one. I babbled on about things far beyond me, made small talk about wonders way over my head. You told me, 'Listen, and let Me do the talking. Let Me ask the questions. You give the answers.' I admit I once lived by rumors of You; now I have it all firsthand—from my own eyes and ears! I'm sorry—forgive me. I'll never do that again, I promise! I'll never again live on crusts of hearsay, crumbs of rumor (Job 42:1-6).

When called to account, in the presence of God will we respond like Job? Will we be quiet and listen to what God has to teach us?
Take your time. Study God's creation.
Next time you happen to descend into the Marianna Trench, notice the arthropods!
Whenever you see an aspen tree, stop and rub its bark.
Give thanks to God for ingeniously, diversely, and sovereignly creating the Marianna Trench and for providing the aspen its own sunscreen.
As you ascend to the surface in your submersible, or as you snowshoe away from the stand of quakies, declare your thanks with the Psalmist—

O Lord, our Lord, how majestic is Your name in all the earth! You have set Your glory above the heavens. From the lips of children and infants You have ordained praise because of Your enemies, to silence the foe and the avenger. When I consider Your heavens, the work of Your fingers, the moon and the stars, which You have set in place, what is man that You are mindful of him, the son of man that You care for him? You made him a little lower than the heavenly beings and crowned him with glory and honor. You made him ruler over the works of Your hands; You put everything under his feet: all flocks and herds, and the beasts of the field, the birds of the air, and the fish of the sea, all that swim the paths of the seas. O Lord, our Lord, how majestic is Your name in all the earth! (Psalm 8:1-9, NIV).

Chapter 2

"Abel: God's Absence"

"The Hero of Faithfulness."
But is God really a Hero?

The easy answer is—what are you talking about? Of course, God is a Hero; to suggest otherwise is the first step toward heresy!

I get that, but have you read Genesis 4 carefully? Close reading and careful thinking might make you wonder about some of God's hero-qualities.

"Adam lay with his wife Eve, and she became pregnant and gave birth to Cain. She said, 'With the help of the Lord I have brought forth a man.' Later she gave birth to his brother Abel" (Genesis 4:1&2, NIV).

Seems straightforward so far. Let's continue—

"Now Abel kept flocks, and Cain worked the soil. In the course of time Cain brought some of the fruits of the soil as an offering to the Lord. But Abel brought fat portions from some of the firstborn of his flock" (Genesis 4:3&4, NIV).

This has to be a good thing—two men bringing offerings to God.

The Lord looked with favor on Abel and his offering, but on Cain and his offering He did not look with favor. So Cain was very angry, and his face was downcast. Then the Lord said to Cain, 'Why are you angry? Why is your face downcast? If you do what is right, will you not be accepted? But if you do not do what is right, sin is crouching at your door; it desires to have you, but you must master it' (Genesis 4:5-7, NIV).

Uh-oh. A tiff between brothers. If the first husband and wife, Adam and Eve, had problems in the Garden of Eden, it is absolutely no surprise that their first children developed a sibling rivalry.

Adam and Eve have two boys. One runs the family livestock operation. The other heads up the farming side of things. Both boys bring offerings to God. One offering is favorable. One offering is not favorable. One brother gets mad, pouts, and takes matters into his own hands.

This might be the first time in human history, but it is a scene that has been and will continue to be replayed countless times across the annals of time to all the corners of the globe. I even saw a Barckholtz family version of a sibling rivalry played out at our breakfast table this morning.

The question is—is God a Hero? Is God really "THE Hero of Faithfulness"?

Let's find out by continuing to read Genesis 4—"Cain said to his brother Abel, 'Let's go out to the field.' And while they were in the field, Cain attacked his brother Abel and killed him. Then the Lord said to Cain, 'Where is your brother Abel?' 'I don't know,' he replied. 'Am I my brother's keeper?'" (Genesis 4:8&9, NIV).

Here is where things get tragic. Big brother Cain took out his anger on little brother Abel and killed him. We aren't told how. We are just told that Cain killed Abel. Was it a rock to the head? A knife to the gut? A hammer-lock and choke-hold? We aren't given details on how Cain's attack unfolded. We just know the results. One brother dead. One brother scarred for all time.

Here comes the biggest question. The premise of this study of Hebrews 11 is that God is "THE Hero of Faithfulness." But how can that be?

Where is God's faithfulness to Abel? Somehow, it seems, God was absent from the killing field Abel was murdered in. How can that absence be called faithfulness?

Just one chapter earlier, in Genesis 3, God ended the first game of hide-and-seek by knowing exactly where Adam and his fig leaves were hiding in the Garden.

But now, God seems to not be present when Abel is attacked and killed by Cain. How can God's absence be a sign of His faithfulness?

To begin wrestling through the concept of God's faithfulness existing through God's absence, let's look at the offerings each man made to God.

Cain—the farmer—brought God an offering of "some of the fruits of the soil" (Genesis 4:3, NIV).

Abel—the stockman—brought God an offering of "fat portions from some of the firstborn of his flocks" (Genesis 4:4, NIV).

In the first three chapters of the Bible, God records two creation accounts and the details of humankind's Fall from Grace.

As Genesis 4 continues the story, there has been no record yet given of what or how or when God desires offerings and worship. Abel and Cain's grain and fat portions are the first acts of worship and offering by men to God recorded in Scripture.

The offering of Abel is accepted by God and the offering of Cain is not accepted by God. Why?

Theories for this include that Cain's gift was grain and fruit, but Abel's was a blood sacrifice. Knowing God would later require Jesus' shed blood to provide restoration, we apply that standard to Cain and Abel. But is that accurate? Or are we skewing our perspective because we live twenty centuries on this side of the cross? What about the original context then and there?

In short enough order, God gave plenty of instructions for all kinds of sacrifices—grain, animal, and otherwise. Somehow, it doesn't make sense that God would reject a grain offering over an animal offering when the desires of God for neither kind of offering had yet been given.

Listen to how Hebrews 11 refers to Abel for clues to God's actions—"By an act of faith, Abel brought a better sacrifice to God than Cain. It was what he believed, not what he brought, that made the difference. That's what God noticed and approved as righteous. After all these centuries, that belief continues to catch our notice" (Hebrews 11:4).

Two things are said about Abel and his offering that leave implications about Cain and his.

- Abel gave his offering "by an act of faith." Implication—Cain's offering was not prompted by faith, but by something else.
- "Abel brought a better sacrifice to God than Cain." Implication—Cain's offering was bad.

"By an act of faith," we are told, Abel made his offering. The "what" and "how much" of the offering is not the determining factor. It is the "how" that distinguishes between Abel's and Cain's offerings.

Cain's offering did not find favor with God because it was not offered from faith. It was offered from his own presumptions. First things first, Cain's worship was on target. He was worshiping God. He was making an offering to God. But Cain presumed God would be pleased with his effort and sweat growing the grain and fruit. Cain presumed God would like his thoughtfulness at giving Him some of the produce. Cain was presuming God would be honored by the mere fact that he was doing something.

On the other hand, Abel's offering found favor with God because he gave it in faith. Abel made no presumptions. Abel humbly and worshipfully brought God an offering from his flocks. Culling from some of the firstborn of his flocks, Abel presented his gift to God.

Note that Abel's offering was not "all the firstborn." It was "some" of the firstborn. Just as Cain gave "some" grain, so Abel gave "some" of the firstborn. The "what" and the "how much" of the offerings were not the determining factors in favorability. Abel's offering found favor because of HOW he gave it to God—in faith and humility.

Hebrews 11 says—"By an act of faith, Abel brought a better sacrifice to God than Cain. It was what he believed, not what he brought, that made the difference. That's what God noticed and approved as righteous. After all these centuries, that belief continues to catch our notice."

We hear the word "better" applied to Abel and we automatically assume the opposite must apply to Cain. Our rapid assumption is that the opposite of "better" is bad, or worse.

However, "better" is a comparative word of degree. When two things are compared the progression is—"good" to "better." Not "better" or "bad." (If anything, it would be "better" or "worse," but that isn't the case either.)

As you consider all this, travel with me from the killing fields of Genesis 4, to a small town a few miles from Jerusalem. Cross a couple thousand years from Abel's graveside to about 30 or so AD.

Jesus had some friends in the town of Bethany who provide a comparison to Cain and Abel for us. In the home of Mary and Martha, we find a pair of sisters who express their relationships to Jesus differently.

One visit to His friends unfolded like this—

As Jesus and His disciples were on their way, He came to a village where a woman named Martha opened her home to Him. She had a sister called Mary, who sat at the Lord's feet listening to what He said. But Martha was distracted by all the preparations that had to be made. She came to Him and asked, 'Lord, don't You care that my sister has left me to do the work by myself? Tell her to help me!' 'Martha, Martha,' the Lord answered, 'you are worried and upset about many things, but only one thing is needed. Mary has chosen what is better, and it will not be taken away from her' (Luke 10:38-42, NIV).

Did you listen carefully to what Jesus actually says? Did you also carefully hear what He doesn't say?

Jesus does say—"Martha, Martha. . . only one thing is needed. Mary has chosen what is better. . ."

Jesus does not say—"Martha, Martha. . . you messed up. Get out of the kitchen! Get over here on the sofa! Mary has chosen what is better and you have chosen what is bad."

Mary, sitting on the floor, situated near Jesus' feet, listening to His teaching, chose better.

Martha, in the kitchen, banging pots and pans, stirring the gravy, salting the mashed potatoes, slicing the brisket, putting Jesus' teaching about service into practiced actions, has also chosen something good.

The degrees are not better and bad. The degrees of choice are good and better.

If we fast forward and return with Jesus to Bethany sometime later, we find Mary and Martha's brother, Lazarus, had died.

In John 11, when Jesus arrives to console His friends, we find both sisters ask Jesus the same question—"'Lord,' Martha said to Jesus, 'if You had been here, my brother would not have died.' . . . When Mary reached the place where Jesus was and saw Him, she fell at His feet and said, 'Lord, if You had been here, my brother would not have died'" (John 11:21, 32, NIV).

The implication made by each sister is that Jesus' absence is the reason for their brother's death. Through whatever means He would have chosen, the sisters both have faith that Jesus could have intervened and spared Lazarus.

Jesus' response to the sisters, and His rationale for waiting three days before arriving at Lazarus' grave, comes in verse 40—"Then Jesus said, 'Did I not tell you that if you believed, you would see the glory of God?'" (John 11:40, NIV).

Keep Jesus' interaction with Mary and Martha in mind as we return to Genesis 4 and Abel's body buried in the blood-moistened dirt of the first killing field.

- Is God—"The Hero of Faithfulness". . . or not?

Mary and Martha raise the question about God's presence—or absence, as the case is perceived to be—impacting events.

Abel's murder brings the same issues of God's presence—or absence, as the case might be perceived to be—to the foreground.

- Was God absent when Cain killed Abel?
- If God was present that day would Abel have been killed?

Listen again to Hebrews 11:4, from *The Message*—"By an act of faith, Abel brought a better sacrifice to God than Cain. It was what he believed, not what he brought, that made the difference. That's what God noticed and approved as righteous. After all these centuries, that belief continues to catch our notice."

Two absolutely crucial words in *The Message* for this entire absence/presence of God issue are—"God noticed. . ."

The Amplified Bible says—"God bore witness..."

The NIV says—"God spoke well of..."

If "God noticed" what Abel did, He could not have been absent.

If "God bore witness," He had to have seen something.

If "God spoke well of," He was present, saw, processed, and testified about what He was there to see.

God noticed Abel's offering and gave witness that the "fat portions" of his firstborn livestock were given by faith. God noticed Cain's offering and gave witness that he gave some of his grain from presumption. God noticed Cain's angry reaction. God spoke well of Abel and told Cain to calm down.

God noticed and He was absolutely present with Abel—from the giving of the offering to Cain's ending of his life.

Jesus' promise as He ascended into heaven has been God's promise from before time—"Surely I am with you always, to the very end of the age" (Matthew 28:20, NIV).

God's presence can never be doubted or called into question. Even when we feel most alone, we can never doubt God's presence. Even when our faith feels most dry and barren, the entirety of the Triune God is with us. God's plan for why He chooses to clearly intervene in one situation, but seemingly does not intervene in another, can never be doubted or called into question.

A few weeks ago, a friend's four-and-a-half-year-old grandson was diagnosed with leukemia. Was God absent the day Benaiah's DNA was created? Was God absent somewhere from conception to birth, or through infancy to diagnosis? Or is it God's plan to use doctors, needles, chemotherapy, and other aspects of this little boy's illness, to somehow bring Himself glory? I say "somehow" because my limited view and small faith can't see any good or better or glory in a little boy enduring a bunch of poking and prodding and nausea and pain. But God can.

And that is the point. God can. God notices. God bears witness. God speaks well of. God is present. Even when to our eyes it appears He is absent, God is present and God has a plan.

The critical factor is this—we think we should be allowed to see everything because we think we can handle everything. Except, only

God actually does know, see, and is wise enough to handle the entire plan.

Quite possibly, Jack Nicholson was correct when he screamed at Tom Cruise from the witness stand in the movie, *A Few Good Men*—"You can't handle the truth!" If we think we can handle "the truth, the whole truth, and nothing but the truth," we are trespassing the same dangerous ground of presumption as Cain.

Lazarus' death provided Jesus the opportunity to glorify His Father by bringing Lazarus out of the grave, even over Mary's protestations—"Lord, by this time he stinketh: for he hath been dead four days" (John 11:39, KJV). So also while Abel's blood was crying for vengeance from beneath the soil of his lonely grave, Cain's act of violence provided God the avenue to honor Abel's faith and to be his "Hero of Faithfulness."

Benaiah's leukemia. . . my father's early death. . . the darkest nights of your soul. . . the most troubling days of your life. . . each are events "The Hero of Faithfulness" notices, is present for, and knows how to use to bring glory and honor and praise to Himself.

Chapter 3

"Enoch: God's Pleasure"

I have clear recollections of our family vacation across the South. The memories are made easy because the climax of the many thousand mile journey with Mom, Dad, and four brothers wedged among all the suitcases, in the family station wagon, was Disneyworld, in Orlando, Florida.

I also have these crystal clear memories of our vacation across the land of Dixie because my leg was in a cast that summer. I broke my ankle the day after school got out! When we got to Disneyworld, I couldn't go on most of the rides because I was being pushed around in a wheelchair!

My most deeply-rooted memory of Disneyworld is of NOT getting to go on Swiss Family Tree House! As a matter of record, on April 19, 1995, when Wendy and I went to Disneyland, the Swiss Family Tree House was the first ride I made her take me on!

As we traveled from Houston to Florida, I can remember visiting several old cemeteries in New Orleans. My Dad loved visiting cemeteries—the older, the better.

Giant oak trees. Spanish moss hanging around everywhere. Cryptic, ghostly mausoleums. Civil War-era headstones. Iron fences with fleur-de-lis around certain family plots. Faded names and dates. Some stones inscribed with anecdotes and notations.

In addition to cemeteries, my Dad also loved reading the obituaries. Growing up, we would open *The Houston Chronicle* and laugh at the euphemisms people employed to cover the fact that someone had died.

- Passed away.
- Entered rest.
- Went fishing in the sky.
- Joined his beloved dog, Spike.

When my Dad died, I had to argue with the newspaper over stating the obvious—Arthur Norman Barckholtz had died. Their policy was to say "passed away," or to employ some other nonsense term of falsely disguised sympathy. Finally, they relented and agreed. My Dad's obituary included the only honest, but most rarely used word—died.

As I set the stage for this chapter with scenes of cemeteries and anecdotes of obituaries, the next person in Hebrews 11 who had his relationship with "The Hero of Faithfulness" recorded is one of the most unique men in history—Enoch.

Enoch is only mentioned three times in the Bible—in Genesis 5:21-24, Jude 14-16, and Hebrews 11:5-6. Three mentions might make Enoch seem like a bit player on Scripture's stage. Three references, however, help highlight specific aspects of Enoch's unique relationship with God. Through these three passages, Enoch can teach us some critical aspects of living by faith with Almighty God.

In Genesis 5, we find these words—

When Enoch was sixty-five years old, he had Methuselah. Enoch walked steadily with God. After he had Methuselah, he lived another 300 years, having more sons and daughters. Enoch lived a total of 365 years. Enoch walked steadily with God. And then one day he was simply gone: God took him (Genesis 5:21-24).

It would be easy to zero in on the mysterious, climax of Enoch's life—"Enoch walked with God; then he was no more, because God took him away" (Genesis 5:24, NIV).

Who wouldn't want to join Enoch on one of the Bible's two most glorious trips into God's presence? (Elijah's fiery chariot ride being the other.) To skip to the great by-and-by, focusing only on where and how Enoch was taken is to miss the example of Enoch's life.

Of all the patriarchs listed in Genesis 5, only Mahalalel (895 years), Lamech (777 years), and Enoch (365 years) lived less than 900 years.

If we troll back through these first five chapters of Genesis, Adam was created and lived in a perfect relationship with God. Included in that relationship was spending quality and quantity time with God in the Garden of Eden. Then came the Fall from Grace, causing Adam and Eve to be banished from the Garden.

Following the Fall, in short order, Abel was murdered and "Cain left the presence of God" (Genesis 4:16, NIV). All the named persons of Scripture in Genesis 1-4 have had their relationships with God ruined by sin.

In Genesis 5, we read the lineage and details of ten patriarchs. From Adam, to Seth, to Enosh, to Kenan, to Mahalalel, to Jared, we are given facts, ages, and lineages. But there are zero specific details given about their relationship to God. That changes with Enoch.

In Genesis 5:21-24, we are given six tidbits of information about Enoch's life—

- At age 65, Enoch had Methuselah.
- Enoch walked steadily with God.
- After Methuselah, Enoch has more kids and lives 300 more years.
- He lived a total of 365 years.
- Enoch walked steadily with God.
- Then he was gone; God took him.

Then the genealogy quickly resumes with Methuselah and Lamech. The pattern returns to facts, ages, and lineages, until Noah comes along.

Here is an intriguing question—

- Why, after nothing but a Joe Friday-like recitation of facts and figures, why the deluge of details on Enoch's life?

When every other patriarch lives about 900 years, to live less than half as long as any of your relatives has to mean something. To have the Holy Spirit inspire Moses to record six specific details of your life has to mean something. There has to be something of major significance for the Holy Spirit to even repeat one detail twice—"Enoch walked steadily with God."

As an aside—repetition is always a piece of critical import in the Bible. There are plenty of things the Holy Spirit could have inspired in God's Word, but chose not to. So pay close attention to details that are repeated. If the Holy Spirit chose to inspire an author to repeat something—PAY ATTENTION! Even more so, PAY ATTENTION to anything in the Bible receiving triple repetition!

Clearly Enoch and God had a special relationship. So special that the Holy Spirit tells us twice that Enoch "walked steadily with God."

If you spend a few minutes sitting on a park bench people-watching, it soon becomes apparent that there are probably innumerable ways to walk. Each walk conjures up a specific image—

- Walked hesitantly—two steps. . . stop. . . look up. . . down. . . around. . . three steps. . . scratch head. . . continue. . .
- Walked drunkenly—one step left. . . one stagger right. . . a lean against a wall. . . arms flailing. . . a trip up the steps. . .
- Walked hurriedly—head down. . . strides long. . . destination dead-ahead. . .
- Walked timidly—a couple steps. . . fingers to the mouth. . . reach for Mom's hand. . . twirl the skirt. . . keep taking small steps. . .

What do you visualize in this picture?

- "Enoch walked steadily with God. . ."

Perhaps some synonyms describing God's walk with Enoch could be—

- Walked contentedly. . .
- Walked peacefully. . .
- Walked passionately. . .
- Walked continuously. . .

Somehow, Enoch experienced something deeper in his relationship with "The Hero of Faithfulness" than the other patriarchs listed in Genesis 5. Enoch's walking steadily with God hearkens back to the beginning. Enoch's walk with God reminds us of God's walking in the Garden of Eden with Adam in the cool of the evening.

Here is something critical to grasp ahold of. In John 14:6-7, Jesus says—"I am the Way and the Truth and the Life. No one comes to the Father except through Me. If you really knew Me, you would know My Father as well. From now on, you do know Him and have seen Him" (John 14:6-7, NIV).

Walking steadily with God, as Enoch, leads us to the most ultimate truth—Jesus Christ died to give us grace and forgiveness.

Walking steadily with God, as Enoch, leads us deeper into fellowship with God that culminates in eternal life.

To learn more about walking steadily with God, let's turn our attention to the second-last Book of the Bible, the Epistle of Jude.

In Jude's little prophecy, the half-brother of Jesus writes—

> Enoch, the seventh from Adam, prophesied about these men: 'See, the Lord is coming with thousands upon thousands of His holy ones to judge everyone, and to convict all the ungodly of all the ungodly acts they have done in the ungodly way, and of all the harsh words ungodly sinners have spoken against Him.' These men are grumblers and faultfinders; they follow their own evil desires; they boast about themselves and flatter others for their own advantage (Jude 14-16, NIV).

Jude reveals that Enoch not only "walked steadily with God," he didn't keep his relationship with God to himself. Enoch spent his 365 years prophesying and teaching about the way to a right relationship with God. Enoch not only told people who to avoid and what to avoid. Enoch told them—more importantly, he showed them through his actions and life choices—how to build a steady relationship with God.

Here is a morsel to chew on—Adam was still alive when Enoch was alive. Adam died when Enoch was about 300 years old. One of the persons Enoch could have learned about walking steadily with God HAD REALLY WALKED IN THE GARDEN OF EDEN WITH GOD! Enoch could have reminded his great-great-great-great-grandfather, Adam, what walking steadily with God looked like!

Knowing God the Father, and showing others the way to God the Father, are the first two pieces of Enoch's faith. The third is revealed in Hebrews 11—

> By an act of faith, Enoch skipped death completely. 'They looked all over and couldn't find him because God had taken him.' We know on the basis of reliable testimony that before he was taken 'he pleased God.' It's impossible to please God apart from faith. And why? Because anyone who wants to approach God must believe both that He exists and that He cares enough to respond to those who seek Him (Hebrews 11:5-6).

Enoch knows God and he shows others the way to God. Enoch also daily goes about living life God's way. Enoch demonstrates for everyone, from Adam to today, how to live a God-pleasing life. Hebrews puts the example in straightforward language—"It is impossible to please God apart from faith" (Hebrews 11:6).

Faith requires an object. Faith is not just a vacuous, empty, feel-good thing.

Specifically, Enoch displays two important components of faith—

- You have to have faith that God really does exist.
- You also have to have faith that God really does love and desire a relationship with His children.

These two things might seem obvious. But are they?

Consider this common misconception about God's existence. Many people view "The Hero of Faithfulness" as some kind of stand-offish, old timekeeper.

Every world religion and spiritual philosophy, as well as many well-intentioned Christians, live with a god who demands you try to earn your way to his good side. Life is about you qualifying through your efforts to exist in god's presence.

However, "The Hero of Faithfulness," the Triune God of the Bible, is not like that. Unique among every approach to faith and things spiritual, the God of the Bible is not some arbitrary, old-school

Russian Olympic judge waiting to smugly post a devilishly low score on your life.

Quite the opposite. The God of the Bible "cares enough to respond to those who seek Him." The God of Hebrews 11 is a God who pursues intimate relationships with His created children. Enoch's God is a very real, present, passionate, living, loving God. The God of the Christian faith wants to cultivate intimate relationships with those who know Him. God wants to see those who know Him, share Him, with others.

For us, studying the Bible's three references to Enoch and God's faithfulness to him, the question becomes—

- How can I live like Enoch?
- How can I have such a special, intimate, passionate relationship with Almighty God through Christ Jesus that God receives pleasure from knowing me?

Paul's prayer in Ephesians 1 is a beautiful starting point for cultivating this kind of steady and God-pleasing walk. Paul writes to his friends in Ephesus—

> For this reason, ever since I heard about your faith in the Lord Jesus and your love for all the saints, I have not stopped giving thanks for you, remembering you in my prayers. I keep asking that the God of our Lord Jesus Christ, the glorious Father, may give you the Spirit of wisdom and revelation, so that you may know Him better. I pray also that the eyes of your heart may be enlightened in order that you may know the hope to which He has called you, the riches of His glorious inheritance in the saints, and His incomparably great power for us who believe (Ephesians 1:15-19a, NIV).

When "the glorious Father of our Lord Jesus" is your personal "Hero of Faithfulness," it is time to rejoice and give thanks!

When Jesus Christ, through the grace and resurrection power of His cross and empty tomb, is your Savior and Lord, it is time to join Paul rejoicing and giving thanks!

From this relationship of grace and joy, the Holy Spirit is ready to pour out His power and love so you are able to walk and live in ways that show wisdom and hope to others! The eyes of your heart are ready to be opened to the reality of helping others see the Way, the Truth, and the Life—Jesus Christ!

The Old Testament prophet Micah provides a series of questions and answers that help the eyes of our hearts to see the way to growing in a God-pleasing relationship like the one Enoch enjoyed with our faithful God.

In *The Message*, Micah 6:6-7 frame four questions like this—

> How can I stand up before God and show proper respect to the high God? Should I bring an armload of offerings topped off with yearling calves? Would God be impressed with thousands of rams, with buckets and barrels of olive oil? Would He be moved if I sacrificed my firstborn child, my precious baby, to cancel my sin? (Micah 6:6-7).

The first question is fairly legitimate—how can I respect and relate to God?

The second and third questions begin to reveal presumptuous answers disguising themselves as questions—will God be pleased with a bunch of possessions and stuff I might deign to give Him? (Think back to Cain for insight on how to answer this one!)

The fourth question shows the depths of depravity to which we are each tempted to fall in the pursuit of any kind of relationship to God—how about if I sacrifice the life of my firstborn child, will that open up a better relationship with God?

The answers to these questions on how to live before God are given in verse 8—"But He's already made it plain how to live, what to do, what God is looking for in men and women. It's quite simple: Do what is fair and just to your neighbor, be compassionate and loyal in your love, And don't take yourself too seriously—take God seriously" (Micah 6:8).

Be fair. Be just. Be compassionate. Be loyal. And this extra special piece of Micah's answer—don't take yourself too seriously.

Let's face it—we take ourselves way too seriously. Our self-righteous preoccupation with looking intense and pious (which really only makes us look constipated!) is a fundamental problem we each need God's grace to overcome. Because the reality is—it is God who is to be taken seriously. We are to be taken lightly.

The NIV casts Micah's answers like this—"[God] has showed you, O man, what is good. And what does the Lord require of you? To act justly and to love mercy and to walk humbly with your God" (Micah 6:8, NIV).

Justice. Mercy. Humility. Fairness. Compassion. Loyalty. All these are key aspects of Enoch's relationship to "The Hero of Faithfulness." "Walk humbly with your God" might be the most precious synonym for describing Enoch's "walking steadily with God."

In the end, Enoch spent 365 years walking humbly and steadily with God. At the end of these years, Enoch not only received the ultimate E-ticket ride into God's presence, he received the greatest possible epitaph one could have engraved on a tombstone—"He pleased God!"

Now what about you?

Motivated by the Holy Spirit's wisdom and revelation of Jesus Christ, will you please God through justice, mercy, and humility?

Inspired by the steady walk of Enoch with God, will you lead others to a mature, steady, passionate, God-pleasing relationship with "The Hero of Faithfulness"?

Chapter 4

"Noah: God's Intimacy"

On October 14, 1066AD, the fortunes of England were at stake. Two armies were racing toward destiny on the battlefield. Descending from the north, following a recent battle against Viking invaders, was the English army under the command of King Harold II. Having finally crossed the English Channel, and attacking from the south, was the Norman-French army led by Duke William II of Normandy.

The battle that ensued took place at Senlac Hill, a few miles outside the town of Hastings. To history, the conflict that day became known as the Battle of Hastings. To most of us, the Battle of Hastings might ring a faint bell from somewhere deep in the recesses of our 8th grade World History memories.

In the battle, King Harold II of England was killed. According to legend, he was shot by an arrow through his eye. The Norman invaders decisively won the battle. In short order, Duke William II became King William I, the first Norman king of England. As his tenure on the throne continued, he became known to his countrymen and to history as William the Conqueror.

Waged almost 950 years ago, the Battle of Hastings was not only a turning point in world history, it also can serve as a reference point for our continuing glance at the lives of the patriarchs listed in Genesis 5.

- Adam lived 930 years...
- Methuselah lived 969 years...
- Noah lived 950 years...

If we imagine these three giants living today, the duration of the lives of these Genesis Patriarchs would have seen them born around the time of the Battle of Hastings! With that as a birth date, they each would have lived until the turn of the 21st century!

Visualize just a few of the monumental events someone born at the Battle of Hastings would have seen across all these centuries—

- The Magna Carta signed in 1215AD
- Columbus' Discovery of the "New World" in 1492AD
- Martin Luther's "95 Theses" in 1517, and the subsequent Protestant Reformation
- Michelangelo, da Vinci, Bach, Galileo, and all the rest of the Renaissance movement
- The American Revolution of 1776
- The French Revolution of 1789
- World Wars I & II
- The inventions of the printing press, the automobile, nuclear energy, and the iPhone

How is that for some perspective of what constitutes a long life!

Here are a few more insights gleaned from the numbers and mathematics of the patriarchs' lives—

- Lamech (Noah's Dad) was about 55 when his great-great-great-great-great-great-grandfather Adam died.
- Enoch was taken to heaven by God at the spritely and youthful age of 365—669 years before the Flood. . . and his son (Lamech) and grandson (Methuselah) almost lived until those waters flowed.
- Lamech lived 777 years. He died only 5 years before the Flood.
- Methuselah, the oldest man in the Bible, lived 969 years. Methuselah died in the year of the Flood, presumably before the waters raged.

In our generation, we used to celebrate with Willard Scott on *The Today Show* the birthdays of 100-year-olds. On the radio, we used to listen each day to Paul Harvey tell us about the longest marriages of our day. Honesty, however, would force us to admit, our perspectives on time and life are limited to our relatively short 70-80 year life-spans.

The Prayer of Moses recorded as Psalm 90 summarizes—

> Lord, You have been our dwelling place throughout all generations. Before the mountains were born or You brought forth the earth and the world, from everlasting to everlasting You are God. You turn men back to dust, saying, 'Return to dust, O sons of men.' For a thousand years in Your sight are like a day that has just gone by, or like a watch in the night. . . All our days pass away under Your wrath; we finish our years with a moan. The length of our days is seventy years—or eighty, if we have the strength; yet their span is but trouble and sorrow, for they quickly pass, and we fly away (Psalm 90:1-4, 9-10, NIV).

When it comes to time, if anyone knew what he was talking about, it was Moses. As the divinely inspired author of both the Book of Genesis and Psalm 90, Moses had the facts, lineages, and timelines firmly in his grasp when he wrote these words—

> Teach us to number our days aright, that we may gain a heart of wisdom. Relent, O Lord! How long will it be? Have compassion on Your servants. Satisfy us in the morning with Your unfailing love, that we may sing for joy and be glad all our days. Make us glad for as many days as You have afflicted us, for as many years as we have seen trouble. May Your deeds be shown to Your servants, Your splendor to their children. May the favor of the Lord our God rest upon us; establish the work of our hands for us—yes, establish the work of our hands (Psalm 90:12-17, NIV).

Unfortunately, following the death of Adam and the glorification of Enoch, "numbering days aright" and being satisfied with God's unfailing love didn't happen. In fact, just the opposite.

The passage of centuries following Enoch's departure saw a swift and slippery slide into degeneracy. So dreadful did things become that God saw all the evil of the world and He declared—

'I'll get rid of My ruined creation, make a clean sweep: people, animals, snakes and bugs, birds—the works. I'm sorry I made them.' . . . As far as God was concerned, the Earth had become a sewer; there was violence everywhere. God took one look and saw how bad it was, everyone corrupt and corrupting—life itself corrupt to the core. . . God was sorry that He had made the human race in the first place; it broke His heart (Genesis 6:7, 11-12, 6).

In this world of sin and evil, Noah lived. From the depths of this depraved and indifferent evil—"Noah was different. God liked what He saw in Noah" (Genesis 6:8).
Take a moment and get a grasp of the scene—

- Everywhere humanity exists, there is evil upon evil, and degeneracy upon degeneracy, always getting worse by the day.
- In the midst of the evil, is one, lone, righteous man named Noah.
- Surrounding Noah is history's first family, including Methuselah and Lamech.

My Grandfather, Paul Mroch, died in 2002, at the age of 93. Although he lived in southern Indiana, and I lived variously in Texas, Nebraska, Missouri, Illinois, or California, I remember several pieces of his advice vividly.

An avid golfer, my Grandpa was a small man. As a result, he was never a big hitter. He did, however, hit the golf ball disgustingly straight down the middle every time. More than once, I can recall him saying (usually while searching the woods to help me find yet another of my spectacularly errant shots)—"It doesn't matter how far you hit the ball, if you can't find it." Gee, thanks, Grandpa!

Grandpa Mroch graduated from Concordia Seminary in 1932. I graduated from the same institution sixty years later, in 1992. Before his health began to fail, we were able to lead worship together one time. Grandpa's comment about my sermon that day was—"At least you had a good text!" Ouch!

At my father's (his son-in-law's) death, Grandpa stood, leaning on his cane, holding the side of the casket, repeating—"That should be me in there."

If I can recall these, and more interactions, with my grandfather spread over just a couple decades, imagine what Noah must have heard and learned from his ancestors—over the centuries of their lives together!

Certainly, from his father Lamech, who was 113 when Enoch was translated from earth to heaven by God, Noah heard account after account of what it meant to "walk steadily with God."

Likewise, from his grandfather Methuselah, Noah had to have heard more than once about the faithfulness of God to his six-great-grandpa, Adam, and to his great-grandpa, Enoch.

As a result of all these years and family interactions, "Noah was a righteous man, blameless among the people of his time, and he walked with God" (Genesis 6:9b, NIV).

Interesting in a literary kind of way that the Scriptures record Noah only "walked with God." No adjectives. No "steadily," as with Enoch. I wonder—is the lack of descriptor a foreshadowing of Noah's drunken, staggering, naked walk to his tent a few hundred years down the road? Speculation only.

With all the corruption and evil, the degradation and sin, swirling around the world and through his neighborhood, God sees Noah's integrity and righteousness. Instead of abolishing the entire creation as He first inclined, God selects Noah to be the focal point for a divine "reset" of the human condition—"So God said to Noah, 'I am going to put an end to all people, for the earth is filled with violence because of them. I am surely going to destroy both them and the earth. So make yourself an ark of cypress wood. . .'" (Genesis 6:13-14a, NIV).

For 100 years, Noah built his arky-arky. For 100 years, Noah searched hither and yon for cypress wood. For 100 years, Noah collected animals and animal feed. For 100 years, Noah sweat in the desert heat building and stocking God's big boat. For 100 years, Noah endured the skepticism and cruelty of the degenerates around the neighborhood. For 100 years, Noah sat down to dinner with his father (Lamech) and his grandfather (Methuselah) and endured their questions about his never-ending building project.

Remarkably, given all the details, time, investment, and scorn coming his way—"Noah did everything just as God commanded him" (Genesis 6:22, NIV).

Talk about a demonstration of faith. For 100 years—

> By faith, Noah built a ship in the middle of dry land. He was warned about something he couldn't see, and acted on what he was told. The result? His family was saved. His act of faith drew a sharp line between the evil of the unbelieving world and the rightness of the believing world. As a result, Noah became intimate with God (Hebrews 11:7).

Talk, also, about a demonstration of God's faithfulness to Noah! God looked around the world and saw Noah. God liked what He saw, so He chose Noah and gave him his assignment. Then, for 100 years, through thick and thin, God faithfully stood by His servant. "As a result, Noah became intimate with God" (Hebrews 11:7). In many ways, that is the greatest lesson to be drawn from Noah's life with God. Noah's faith and—even greater—God's faithfulness to Noah led to a century-long (and then for 350 more years after the Flood!) relationship based on God's intimacy.

Even though he was filled with integrity and righteousness, Noah was surrounded by depravity and sin. In spite of the encouragement that undoubtedly came from hearing of Enoch's steady walk with God, Noah had to endure decades of jeers and haranguing from his evil onlookers. Throughout this all this, Noah enjoyed intimacy with God.

Imagine what this must have been like for Noah—

- After a long day looking for giraffe food and that elusive female gorilla, Noah comes home, and God says, "Good work."
- After another day cutting cypress boards, while the neighbors sat around drinking and jeering at him, and God says, "Thank you."

Day in and year out, Noah labored and God was intimately faithful to him.

Because I am probably more like Noah's sinful and rebellious neighbors—wanting to take cheap shots at all the animals and smells and oddities on the ark—we are going to jump from Noah's 100-year building project to his first encounter with God after the floodwaters rose, fell, receded, and the dove flew away.

After everyone left the ark for recently dried land, Noah immediately set up an altar and offered a sweet-smelling sacrifice to God. From His throne above, God looked at Noah and his family and in an act of pure intimacy, God blessed them.

God also told Noah and his family—

I now establish My covenant with you and with your descendants after you and with every living creature that was with you—the birds, the livestock and all the wild animals, all those that came out of the ark with you—every living creature on earth. I establish My covenant with you: Never again will all life be cut off by the waters of a flood; never again will there be a flood to destroy the earth (Genesis 9:9-11, NIV).

God then sealed His covenant with a gift of immense majesty and beauty—the rainbow.

God created rainbows to remind us of His intimacy with us. Of an even greater magnitude, rainbows are meant to remind God of His faithfulness to Himself.

The millions of water droplets gathered together, each refracting a band of the sun's light, reveal the beautiful colors of the spectrum. From red to orange, indigo to violet, rainbows are Divine gifts to remind God of His gracious covenant promise to us. Never again will God bring judgment via a flood. Instead grace and life flow from the water and blood of Jesus' pierced side.

Because of Jesus' blood and righteousness, we also can have intimacy with God. While we might have to figure out God's desires for our lives, we can rest easy knowing God has promised to never to cover the world with another Flood.

Consider what Noah did, one more time—

- Build an ark.
- Bring animals on it.
- Store food for a long voyage.

- Do this in the desert.
- Do this without rain.
- Oh. . . and this little project. . . will take you 100 years to complete.

The most telling sign of Noah's faith is in Genesis 6:22—"Noah did everything just as God commanded him" (Genesis 6:22, NIV).

The most amazing aspect of God's faithfulness to Noah is in Hebrews 11:7—"As a result, Noah became intimate with God" (Hebrews 11:7).

That same intimacy with God is ours through Jesus. Remember that next time you spot a rainbow arcing across the sky!

Chapter 5

Abram: God's Call

*J*ust to date myself...

I can remember the crowning moment to all the plans for our honeymoon. Reservations at the Excalibur in Las Vegas and at the Grand Canyon had been made. Routes from Idaho to Texas via 4 Corners, White Sands, and Big Bend National Park had been figured. Finally, it was time to go the local AAA office to buy travelers checks and to get a Triptik.

Some of you are scratching your heads wondering what I am talking about—travelers checks?

Others of you are nodding as a wave of nostalgia washes over you—oh yes, the Triptik...

The year was all the way back in the last millennia—1991. Before debit cards and ATMs. Long before smart phone apps (including the AAA Triptik app). Back in the dark ages before disembodied voices saying, "Turn left in one-quarter mile." Before even Google maps, Yahoo! Maps, or MapQuest. In those most ancient of days, AAA would print out a flip card book charting your desired route across the country. Ahhh... the privileges of membership!

I heard this sentiment expressed recently—"You have to know where you are going to prepare to get there."

At first blush, that seems to be an obvious statement—"You have to know where you are going to prepare to get there."

But is it true?

If you don't know where you are going, what clothes do you take? Swimsuits or snow skis? Golf clubs or knitting needles? Both? Neither? All of the above? How do you decide?

If you don't know where you are going, how will you know what address to plug into your GPS? Or your smartphone? Or MapQuest?

The next Old Testament patriarch spoken of in Hebrews 11 gets straight to the heart of knowing how to get where God wants you to be.

In *The Message*, Hebrews 11:8 says—"By an act of faith, Abraham said yes to God's call to travel to an unknown place that would become his home. When he left he had no idea where he was going. . ." (Hebrews 11:8).

All the energy we expend preparing, planning, and controlling our lives, oftentimes pigeonholes the Holy Spirit's freedom to act. Our need for security and safety nets, frequently shackles God's call to action and movement in our lives.

Back before he became Abraham—"The Father of Many Nations"—God spoke to a man named, simply, Abram. In Genesis 12—"The Lord had said to Abram, 'Leave your country, your people and your father's household and go to the land I will show you'" (Genesis 12:1, NIV).

With no Triptik, no GPS, no disembodied voice (at least, I don't think the voice of the Lord would sound disembodied!)—

> Abram left, as the Lord had told him; and Lot went with him. Abram was seventy-five years old when he set out from Haran. He took his wife Sarai, his nephew Lot, all the possessions they had accumulated and the people they had acquired in Haran, and they set out for the land of Canaan, and they arrived there (Genesis 12:4-5, NIV).

But the land of Canaan wasn't the be all and end all of this journey—

> Abram traveled through the land as far as the site of the great tree of Moreh at Shechem. At that time the Canaanites were in the land. . . From there he went on toward the hills east of

Bethel and pitched his tent, with Bethel on the west and Ai on the east. There he built an altar to the Lord and called on the name of the Lord. Then Abram set out and continued toward the Negev. Now there was a famine in the land, and Abram went down to Egypt. . . (Genesis 12:6, 8-10, NIV).

Abram's entire journey from Haran, through Canaan, to Egypt, came about as a result of two things—God's call and Abram's trust.

Re-read. . . pause. . . and contemplate carefully. . . God's call to Abram—"The Lord had said to Abram, 'Leave your country, your people and your father's household and go to the land I will show you'" (Genesis 12:1, NIV).

Put yourself in Abram's sandals. . .

- "Leave your country"—okay. . . but. . . let me ask. . . do I get to pick my next destination? If so, I would prefer landing in England, Ireland, the Bahamas, or Australia. No way am I leaving here to go to India, Mexico, or Haiti.
- "Leave your family"—no problem, especially if you mean crazy Uncle Al and some of my sketchy cousins.
- "Leave your father's home"—Picture Abram, scratching his beard, mumbling to himself, "I am 75. Maybe it is about time. Then again, Sarah's mutton stew is nowhere as good as my mom's."
- "Leave. . . for a land I will show you"—what do you mean? Where am I going? How will I get there? How long will we stay? Where will we settle down?

Ahh. . . settling. . .

This is really one of our most critical questions when it comes to responding to God's call and to God's leading—

- Where are You leading?
- How long will it take?
- And, how soon can I settle down and retire from following?

THE Hero of Faithfulness

One of the Bible's saddest chapters closes right before God calls Abram in Genesis 12. Read the end of Genesis 11—

> Terah took his son Abram, his grandson Lot son of Haran, and his daughter-in-law Sarai, the wife of his son Abram, and together they set out from Ur of the Chaldeans to go to Canaan. But when they came to Haran, they settled there. Terah lived 205 years, and he died in Haran (Genesis 11:31-32).

Visualize the scene—Terah set out for Canaan. Terah followed the route from Ur. Terah went a long way along the way. Terah got as far as Haran. Then, Terah settled. Terah lived over two hundred more years. Then, he died.

That whole litany sounds deflating. From an expectant beginning, to a fork in the road. From Ur to Canaan, but. . .

What was it about Haran that distracted Terah? What caused him to stop short of Canaan, his goal? What made Terah settle in Haran?

"But when they got as far as Haran, they settled. . ." It sounds incomplete. Like a pregnant pause that never delivers. "Terah. . . set out from Ur. . . but when they got as far as Haran, they settled. . ."

When you settle short of the destination, you will not reach God's goal for you!

When you settle short of where God is leading, you will not reach God's fullest hopes and desires for you!

"So Abram went, as the Lord had told him. . ." (Genesis 12:4, ESV).

Check out the verbs marking Abram's journey—

- Abram went. . . (v.4)
- Abram took. . . (v.5)
- Abram set out to go to. . . (v.5)
- Abram passed through. . . (v.6)
- Abram built there an altar. . . (v.7)
- Abram moved on from there. . . (v.8)
- Abram pitched his tent. . . (v.8)
- Abram built an altar and call on the name of the Lord. . . (v.8)
- Abram journeyed on, still going toward. . ." (v.9)
- Abram went down to Egypt. . . (v.10)

God called Abram from the only land and family he had ever known, to follow Him to an unknown land. Abram trusted God and followed Him across Canaan, through the desert, to a temporary time in Egypt. (Temporary if you read ahead to Genesis 13—"So Abram left Egypt. . .")

God called. Abram trusted.

God led. Abram followed.

God led some more. Abram followed some more.

Which leaves us with two huge questions—

- How do we know God's call?
- And, how do we come up with the trust to follow God's call?

And, I guess, a third great question—

- How do we keep following God's call (like Abram) and not settle (like Terah)?

We would like to believe knowing God's call is as easy as answering the phone.

Your personal ringtone sounds (something exciting like the sweet guitar riff at the beginning of Rush's *Spirit of the Radio*). You answer, "Hello. . ."

God (sounding more like James Earl Jones, than the Verizon Wireless guy) says, "Can you hear me now? Go and do this."

We would like God's call on our lives to be this clear and direct.

Oswald Chambers, in *My Utmost for His Highest*, describes something quite different, however—"Get out of your mind the idea of expecting God to come with compulsions and pleadings. When our Lord called His disciples there was no irresistible compulsion from outside."[1]

We would (arrogantly?) like to think God will raise Himself from some depths far below us, onto our exalted pedestal, to beg and plead with us to serve Him.

Instead, the reality is much more simple and subtle. Listen to the encounter between God and Isaiah, recorded in Isaiah 6—

> In the year that King Uzziah died, I saw the Lord seated on a throne, high and exalted, and the train of His robe filled the temple. Above Him were seraphs, each with six wings: With two wings they covered their faces, with two they covered their feet, and with two they were flying. And they were calling to one another: 'Holy, holy, holy is the Lord Almighty; the whole earth is full of His glory.' At the sound of their voices the doorposts and thresholds shook and the temple was filled with smoke. 'Woe to me!' I cried. 'I am ruined! For I am a man of unclean lips, and I live among a people of unclean lips, and my eyes have seen the King, the Lord Almighty.' Then one of the seraphs flew to me with a live coal in his hand, which he had taken with tongs from the altar. With it he touched my mouth and said, 'See, this has touched your lips; your guilt is taken away and your sin atoned for.' Then I heard the voice of the Lord saying, 'Whom shall I send? And who will go for us?' And I said, 'Here am I. Send me!' (Isaiah 6:1-8, NIV).

God brought Isaiah into a vision of His heavenly throne room. God cleansed Isaiah from the impurities of his own sin. And God laid a question before Isaiah—"Who will go for Us?"

There was no demand. There was no destination. There was no timeline, or 5-year plan. There was also no compulsion or negotiation or bartering or haranguing. There was just the question—"Whom shall I send, and who will go for Us?"

It was up to Isaiah to respond and say—"Here I am. Send me!"

Again, listen to Oswald Chambers—

> God did not address the call to Isaiah; Isaiah overheard God saying, "Who will go for us?" The call of God is not for the special few, it is for everyone. . . It is not a question of God singling out a man and saying, "Now, *you* go." God did not lay a strong compulsion on Isaiah; Isaiah was in the presence of God and he overheard the call, and realized that there was nothing else for him but to say, in conscious freedom, "Here am I, send me."[2]

All of this leads to the second great question concerning God's call—

- How do we come up with the trust to answer and follow God's call?

The answer—you don't. I don't. We don't conjure up trust by some great inner fortitude or strength.

Not only that—you can't. I can't, either. Not only don't we conjure our own trust, we can't manufacture trust. We are completely incapable of generating the ability to trust and follow God on our own. It is not possible for us to summon the internal will power to trust and follow God by ourselves. That is the job of the Holy Spirit.

Again, Oswald Chambers—"If we let the Spirit of God bring us face to face with God, we too shall hear something akin to what Isaiah heard, the still small voice of God; and in perfect freedom will say, 'Here am I; send me.'"[3]

Letting the Spirit of God speak and guide your life is not like listening to the passionless, disembodied voice of your car's GPS unit—

- "In 15 minutes, share Christ with the lady in the pink hat, drinking a decaf latte, on the front deck of the coffee shop..."
- "In 4 years, go to an orphanage in the Congo and save seven starving children..."
- "Destination missed... recalculating God's goal for your life..."

Listening to the Spirit of God speak and call you to service is more akin to hearing what a pastor friend called the "gentle whisper" of the Lord's voice that Elijah heard on the mountainside—

'Go out and stand on the mountain in the presence of the Lord, for the Lord is about to pass by.' Then a great and powerful wind tore the mountains apart and shattered the rocks before the Lord, but the Lord was not in the wind. After the wind there was an earthquake, but the Lord was not in the earthquake. After the earthquake came a fire, but the Lord was not in the fire. And after the fire came a gentle whisper. When

Elijah heard it, he pulled his cloak over his face and went out and stood at the mouth of the cave. Then a voice said to him, 'What are you doing here, Elijah?' (I Kings 19:11-13, NIV).

In your life, God's call will probably come with no fireworks, or standing ovations. Knowing you are following the call of God and the Holy Spirit of God by trust and faith in Jesus Christ will likely result in a quiet, inner confidence—a "wee small whisper"—that is God preparing to say, "Well, done, good and faithful servant!" (Matthew 25:21, NIV).

Which leaves the third great question. After discerning God's call and responding with the trust and action of the Holy Spirit to God's call—

- How do we keep following God's call and not settle?

Terah followed for quite a ways. It is no small or insignificant journey to travel from Ur to Haran—especially on foot. But then Terah stopped short of Canaan. He settled in Haran and lived out his days there.

Abram followed God from Haran to Canaan and he kept following. He pitched a temporary tent and then kept going again. He landed in Egypt for a time and, even then, Abram kept following wherever God led him.

How do we live out God's call on our lives like Abram and not like Terah?

As I was searching the Internet for driving directions for a recent trip, I used MapQuest's website. At the end of the directions, MapQuest printed this lengthy disclaimer—

> Directions and maps are informational only. We make no warranties on the accuracy of their content, road conditions or route usability or expeditiousness. You assume all risk of use. MapQuest and its suppliers shall not be liable to you for any loss or delay resulting from your use of MapQuest. Your use of MapQuest means you agree to our Terms of Use.

These 62-words were followed by 18 pages explaining MapQuest's "Terms of Use" and "Third Party Notices and Licenses." I couldn't even get the untold number of pages of their "Privacy Conditions" to load.[4]

All these words and all this mumbo-jumbo from MapQuest's legal department to basically say—"You can't trust us to safely get you where you want to go!"

Not so with God's call.

When God calls us, and when the Spirit of God guides us, we are filled with the fruits of the Spirit for the journey.

Remember these fruits?

Paul describes them like this—

But the fruit of the Spirit is love, joy, peace, patience, kindness, goodness, faithfulness, gentleness and self-control. Against such things there is no law. Those who belong to Christ Jesus have crucified the sinful nature with its passions and desires. Since we live by the Spirit, let us keep in step with the Spirit (Galatians 5:22-25, NIV).

Belonging to Jesus, we are called by God to follow—even (especially!) into unknown circumstances. Belonging to Jesus, we are nourished and guided by the Holy Spirit. Our passions and desires are Godly—love, joy, peace, patience, kindness, goodness, faithfulness, gentleness, and self-control. Called by God and belonging to Jesus, we can "keep in step with the Spirit" (Galatians 5:25, NIV) as we journey along. One day after another. One interaction after another. One step after another.

By faith, we can respond to the call of "The Hero of Faithfulness" like Abram, who "when called to go to a place he would later receive as his inheritance, obeyed and went, even though he did not know where he was going" (Hebrews 11:8, NIV).

Is that your ringtone I hear? God is calling.

Are you ready to respond?

Are you set to go?

Chapter 6

Sarah: God's Joy

*H*ere is an oft-quoted, but unsubstantiated statistic—the average 4-year-old laughs 300-400 times a day. However, the typical 40-year-old laughs less than fifteen times a day. This statistic has an almost "urban legend" character to it.[1]

Supposedly, kids laugh up to 400 times a day. Adults, on the other hand, are so uptight they laugh less than fifteen times a day.

This statistic is used to draw many different conclusions.

- The innocence of childhood versus the complexity of adulthood.
- The way seriousness crowds out light-heartedness.
- Conflict between pessimism and optimism.
- Viewing life with a glass half-full or half-empty.
- Despair triumphing over hope.
- Loss conquering triumph.
- The mind subduing emotions.

Regardless of the specific data (or lack thereof?) behind this laughter statistic, it doesn't take an overly generous government stimulus check to conduct a lengthy research project to conclude that there clearly is more laughter on a playground of 4-year-olds, than in a corporate Board Room filled with adults. And, I don't believe it is much of a stretch to say—where there is laughter, there is joy.

Continuing to journey through Hebrews 11, verses 11&12 take us into the heart of one of God's greatest attributes—His joy.

Read these verses about the first woman spoken of in Hebrews 11—

By faith, barren Sarah was able to become pregnant, old woman as she was at the time, because she believed the One who made a promise would do what He said. That's how it happened that from one man's dead and shriveled loins there are now people numbering into the millions (Hebrews 11:11-12).

As we leave Abram's side of the marriage to focus on "barren Sarah," consider what we know of her life—

- When 75-year-old Abram up and left Haran to follow where God led, he took Sarah (or as she was known then, Sarai, his wife, with him (see Genesis 12:4-6).
- After their lengthy journey, and upon their arrival in Egypt, Abram passed Sarah off as his sister because she was a 65-year-old beauty queen. Abram feared the Egyptians would kill HIM because of HER beauty (see Genesis 12:14-20).
- When Abram and Sarah returned later to Bethel, they separated from the only relatives they still had in the country—Lot and his family (see Genesis 13:8-12).
- Abram received a promise from God of "countless" descendants (see Genesis 15:13-16).
- Years went by following this promise with no children. Finally, Sarah gave her handmaid, Hagar, to Abram, and Hagar quickly (or so it seems) conceived and bore a son, Ishmael (see Genesis 16:1-4).
- When Abram was 99, God renewed His promise of a child who would be born to Abram and Sarah (see Genesis 17:15-19).
- Still more time went by and Sarah remained barren. Ishmael also continued to grow. All this time, God kept renewing—but not delivering on—His promise (see Genesis 18:11-15).
- Even though she was post-menopausal and he had "shriveled loins," as Hebrews 11 puts it, for a second time Abraham passed Sarah off as his sister to King Abimelech (see Genesis 20:1-5).

Having taken stock of Sarah's situation, if this were your life story, and your phone rang during supper one evening, how would you respond to the telemarketer asking survey questions like—

- "Is there joy in your life?"
- "How many times have you laughed today?"
- "How frequently have you laughed in the past year?"
- "Do you laugh more or less today than you did ten years ago?"
- "When is the last time you were overwhelmed with a sense of joy?"
- "For demographic purposes only, what is your age, gender, annual income, and firstborn child's blood type?"

You have traveled all over the countryside, from Ur to Egypt and back again, for the better part of a quarter-century. You have listened to God. . . you are still listening to God. You have followed God. . . you are still following God. You have trusted God. . . you are still trusting God. But God just keeps repeating the same outlandish promise about having offspring so numerous they will outshine and outnumber the stars in the heavens.

Yet you remain barren.

Given your age and history, what on earth do you have to laugh—or be joyful—about?

Fortunately, the example of Sarah in Hebrews 11 is another experience in God's unsurpassed faithfulness to His promises.

Throughout their ordeal, Abraham and Sarah maintained faith that God would keep His promise.

When would God's promise be kept? Not soon enough to suit their fancy, so Abraham and Sarah used Hagar to manipulate God's timing. Talk about an unmitigated disaster! Taking matters into their own hands did not work out so well.

How God would keep His Word? If not through Hagar, they had no clue.

However, "The Hero of Faithfulness," in His time and in His fashion, did, ultimately, keep His promise—

Now the Lord was gracious to Sarah as He had said, and the Lord did for Sarah what He had promised. Sarah became pregnant and bore a son to Abraham in his old age, at the very time God had promised him. Abraham gave the name Isaac to the son Sarah bore him. When his son Isaac was eight days old, Abraham circumcised him, as God commanded him. Abraham was a hundred years old when his son Isaac was born to him. Sarah said, 'God has brought me laughter, and everyone who hears about this will laugh with me.' And she added, 'Who would have said to Abraham that Sarah would nurse children? Yet I have borne him a son in his old age.' The child grew and was weaned, and on the day Isaac was weaned Abraham held a great feast (Genesis 21:1-8, NIV).

In this entire saga—from Abraham, to Sarah, including the irrational detour with Hagar and Ishmael, to Isaac—we can see a window into the heart of God. The NIV says, "Now the Lord was gracious to Sarah. . ." This grace of God to "barren Sarah" takes us to the core of His Being.
I John 4 says—

Dear friends, let us love one another, for love comes from God. Everyone who loves has been born of God and knows God. Whoever does not love does not know God, because God is love. This is how God showed His love among us: He sent His one and only Son into the world that we might live through Him. This is love: not that we loved God, but that He loved us and sent His Son as an atoning sacrifice for our sins (I John 4:7-10, NIV).

At the core of God's Being, His greatest attribute is love. God's love sent Jesus Christ to be our Savior. God's love for us comes because of who He is, not who we are. God is love.
Chew on that for a little while. We like to believe God loves us because of who we are. But the reality is that God loves us because of WHO HE IS!

The unsurpassed and unsurpassing greatness of God's love is closely linked to His overwhelming joy and laughter—"But You, God, break out laughing; You treat the godless nations like jokes. Strong God, I'm watching You do it, I can always count on You. God in dependable love shows up on time, shows me my enemies in ruin" (Psalm 59:8-10).

The "Liner Notes" on Psalm 59 tell us David wrote these words at a time when Saul had surrounded David's house in an attempt to kill him. From the midst of his own trial and struggle, David sounds like Sarah—joyful and laughing. In the face of their difficulties, God is faithful to both David and to Sarah.

Guess what? The same is also true for you in your trials. God is faithful to you! God is looking into your circumstance and seeking how to bring joy and laughter into your specific situation.

Whatever (or whoever) it is that you are dealing with, God is faithful. Not only is God faithful to you in your difficulty, I am certain you did not plan to undergo these trials. None of us plan difficulties into our lives. Trials and testings are things that happen. They are certainly not things we plan.

No one wakes up in the morning and says—

- "I think I'll have a stroke today. . ."
- "Today is a great day to become estranged from my daughter. . ."
- "I know! We haven't lost everything in a house fire recently. . ."

Just as you and I don't plan our trials and struggles, so also Sarah never planned on being barren.

As a little girl, Sarah didn't play with her dolls and dream, "Someday I'm never going to have a baby. . ."

While she was dating Abram, Sarah didn't fold and re-fold the baby clothes in her hope chest thinking, "I can't wait to never use these. . ."

Sarah's barrenness was her trial. Seeing others in their community have babies, while she never did, was her burden. Watching even Hagar—Sarah's own servant—relatively easily conceive and have a baby with Abraham—her own husband, with her express consent—was Sarah's cross. Clearly, the problem was in her reproductive system and not Abraham's.

"Now the Lord was gracious to Sarah as He had said, and the Lord did for Sarah what He had promised. Sarah became pregnant and bore a son to Abraham in his old age, at the very time God had promised him" (Genesis 21:1-2, NIV).

"By faith, barren Sarah was able to become pregnant, old woman as she was at the time, because she believed the One who made a promise would do what He said" (Hebrews 11:11).

Guess what? God keeps His promises!

Guess what else? God absolutely loves to keep His promises! Keeping His promises brings God infinite measures of joy and laughter! As a matter of fact, God specializes in bringing joy to Himself so He can rattle heaven's rafters with laughter. God's greatest pleasure comes from keeping the most outrageous of promises.

- Sarah—think you are too old to have a baby? Not so fast! (see Genesis 18:10-15)
- Israelites—think there is no food in the wilderness for all of you to eat? How about quail as far as you can see? (see Numbers 11:30-34)
- Joshua—think those walls of Jericho are too tall and thick to fall down? Not! (see Joshua 6:1-20)
- Elijah—think that widow's jar of oil will run out? Not with Me supplying the oil! (see 1 Kings 17:7-16)

The greater the degree of human impossibility, the greater the amount of joy and laughter God revels in upon accomplishing what we called impossible.

- Noah—ever wonder whether you built the Ark big enough for all the animals? (see Genesis 7:1-10)
- David—ever think you were too small, or Goliath too big? (see 1 Samuel 17)
- Paul—ever have questions about how to survive a snakebite? (see Acts 28:1-6)

Our "Hero of Faithfulness" specializes in finding humor and laughter and joy in the most impossible of all earthly situations.

- No world even exists? "Let there be light... and there was light" (Genesis 1:3, NIV).
- Mary, your virginity is not a problem for Me because "nothing is impossible with God" (Luke 1:37, NIV).
- "Lazarus, come out!" Being four days dead barely causes God's power grid to register a slight flicker. (John 11:43, NIV)
- Ladies, "He is not here; He has risen, just as He said" Crucifixion, death, and burial have no possible mastery over Jesus! (Matthew 28:5, NIV)

Each day, ordinary life teaches us a little bit more about how to deal with and face our struggles. Over the course of time, philosophy and spirituality help us grow a bit more calm in the midst of trials. However, only faith given by grace from "The Hero of Faithfulness," through the power of the Holy Spirit, shows us how to be truly joyful in adversity.

By her own wisdom and strength, Sarah would have had every right to become a bitter, lonely, old lady. By God's grace through faith though, "Sarah said, 'God has brought me laughter, and everyone who hears about this will laugh with me... Who would have said to Abraham that Sarah would nurse children? Yet I have borne him a son in his old age'" (Genesis 21:6-7, NIV).

I don't know your burden. I don't know your trial. I am sure you have them. I have them. We all do.

I don't know the stresses of your situation, but I do know God's promises—

- "God has said, 'Never will I leave you; never will I forsake you.' So we say with confidence, 'The Lord is my helper; I will not be afraid. What can man do to me?'... Jesus Christ is the same yesterday and today and forever" (Hebrews 13:6-8, NIV).
- "Be strong and courageous. Do not be afraid or terrified because of them, for the Lord your God goes with you; He will never leave you nor forsake you" (Deuteronomy 31:6, NIV).
- "No one will be able to stand up against you all the days of your life. As I was with Moses, so I will be with you; I will never leave you nor forsake you... Have I not commanded you? Be

strong and courageous. Do not be terrified; do not be discouraged, for the Lord your God will be with you wherever you go" (Joshua 1:5&9, NIV).

From the midst of hardship and trial, when you struggle to feel certain that God is really with you, remember God's timing and faithfulness to "barren Sarah."

From the dark nights of despair, when you are tempted to doubt because God seems distant and you feel forgotten, reach into your treasure chest.

What?

You heard me correctly—reach into your treasure chest!

Whether a literal chest kept at the end of your bed, or a shelf in your office, or a box in the garage, or even a vibrant corner of your mind, every follower of Jesus Christ should keep a treasure chest. Everyone should keep reminders—both physical items and special memories—from the times you KNEW God was present and active in your life.

Take a look at what Samuel did after subduing the Philistines at the Battle of Mizpah. Samuel "took a stone and set it up between Mizpah and Shen. He named it *Ebenezer*, saying, 'Thus far has the Lord helped us'" (1 Samuel 7:12, NIV, italics in original).[2]

Here is the key to finding joy and laughter in times of trial—know your *Ebenezers*. Keep track of your reminders of God's action during the previous impossible-become-possible times of your life. Keep real, tangible, touchable items and put them in your treasure chest.

What are your *Ebenezers*? What are your personal reminders that "thus far has the Lord helped" you? What reminders do you have from your past that God will keep bringing joy and laughter to you as you go on further into the future?

Keep your *Ebenezers*. Treasure them. Look at them. Take them off the shelf, or out of the treasure chest, and laugh at the memories of God's faithfulness that they bring.

I have a slice of wood I chain-sawed from a downed oak tree in Baton Rouge, Louisiana. This piece of wood reminds me of God's blessing as Buster and I spent a week helping clean up the mess left behind by Hurricanes Ike and Gustav.

I have an unopened jar of Gongura Sauce I purchased in Chennai, India. This jar of sauce reminds me of a plate of mutton so spicy-hot it blistered my lips! It also reminds me of the beads of sweat running down Chuck's face as he tried to eat his dinner! My Gongura *Ebenezer* helps me remember God's continual grace while traveling on a mission trip to India.

I keep a baseball cap from the Mexican League soccer team Cruz Azul as a reminder of the impossible situation faced by a boy I met in Tijuana—God be with Chewey!

I also have joy and laughter and *Ebenezer* stories attached to a can of Spam, some colorful Sharpies, and many other items in my treasure chest. Each one gives me joy and a chuckle as I think back on God's gracious presence at various points in my life.

What are your *Ebenezers*?

What is in your treasure chest?

What reminders do you have of God's grace and presence and timing and joy and laughter during previous impossible events in your life?

What brings you laughter as you embrace God's grace in the midst of your trials?

One day not so long ago, while I was working a part-time job washing windows, I was on the outside of a kitchen window, while my partner was inside. As we were grousing through the open window about the job, I looked down and realized my hand was resting on a decoration the homeowner had sitting on her windowsill. It was a woodcut of one word—LAUGH!

Talk about God's timing, grace, and presence!

Are you going to grouse and be bitter? Or are you going to be filled with His joy and laughter?

Psalm 126 captures the joy and laughter of celebrating God's goodness in impossible situations—

> It seemed like a dream, too good to be true, when God returned Zion's exiles. We laughed, we sang, we couldn't believe our good fortune. We were the talk of the nations—'God was wonderful to them!' God was wonderful to us; we are one happy people. And now, God, do it again—bring rains

to our drought-stricken lives So those who planted their crops in despair will shout hurrahs at the harvest, So those who went off with heavy hearts will come home laughing, with armloads of blessing (Psalm 126:1-6).

Interlude

God's Sovereignty

*H*ere is one of the great conundrums of the Christian faith—

- Bible verses are easy to spit out. . . but what does it take to live out those same verses?

In other words, it is easy to memorize Bible verses and Bible stories. Putting the Bible into practice is another thing altogether. Especially in 21st century America, it is easy to get your hands on a Bible and it is fairly simple to get verses and stories from the Bible into your head. However, it is much more challenging to get the Word of God into the emotions of your heart and the actions of your hands.

Throughout this first section of Hebrews 11, we have seen some of the great patriarchs of the early chapters of Genesis in action. It is easy to spit out their names and re-live their stories—Abel, Enoch, Noah, Abram, Sarah.

When the litany of biblical characters in Hebrews 11 continues in verse 17, the names and stories will remain among the most famous—Abraham, Isaac, Jacob, Joseph, Moses, the Red Sea, Jericho's Wall, Rahab.

In the life and story of each individual or event, we, eventually, arrive at the same tension point—

- How are these followers of God able to know God and to live out their faith?

In each case, the answer is the same—

- Only by the grace and faithfulness of the Triune God to them.
- Only by the sovereign power and presence of Almighty God to them.

Reflect back over the lives we have seen so far. Think again about "barren Sarah," who we just saw in the last chapter. Through all the travails of her life, God remained faithful to His promises. God also remained faithful to her. In her old age, Sarah's womb was opened. She felt the overwhelming joy of childbirth as she brought Isaac, the child whose name, literally, means "Laughter," into the world.

Even from trials and tribulations, God brings laughter and joy to the lives of His children. He gives grace so His followers can live out their faith. God's grace reveals itself in our lives so we can bring Him glory. God's sovereign grace also equips our hearts and hands to help bring others into a living relationship with Him.

As we arrive at Hebrews 11:13, the Holy Spirit-inspired writer pauses, as it were, to reflect on the faith of the men and women he has talked about so far—

> Each one of these people of faith died not yet having in hand what was promised, but still believing. How did they do it? They saw it way off in the distance, waved their greeting, and accepted the fact that they were transients in this world. People who live this way make it plain that they are looking for their true home. If they were homesick for the old country, they could have gone back any time they wanted. But they were after a far better country than that—heaven country (Hebrews 11:13-15).

Each one—Adam, Enoch, Sarah—lived by faith.

Each one—Abel, Noah, Abram—lived with hope in the future fulfillment of God's promises.

These patriarchs each saw God and each one trusted God's pledge to bring forgiveness and restoration to them at some future day. From Adam to Sarah, each individual lived in a personal relationship with the

Triune God. Eventually, each one died with faith that "The Hero of Faithfulness" would be faithful to Himself and to them.

For this faith—"You can see why God is so proud of them, and has a City waiting for them" (Hebrews 11:16).

Stop and think about those words. Re-read these words a couple more times—

- "You can see why God is so proud of them, and has a City waiting for them. . ."

I said read these words a couple more times!
Slowly!
It would be easy for us to jump to the "City waiting for them" part of the verse. After all, we are quick to focus on the eternal glory promised there. Knowing Jesus, we would each like to jump from here to heaven.

However, don't jump past the first part of verse 16—"You can see why God is so proud of them. . ."

Other versions say—"Therefore God is not ashamed to be called their God. . ." (Hebrews 11:16a, NIV).

Whether cast from the negative—"God is not ashamed. . ."—or from the positive—"God is so proud. . ."—this is a remarkable statement!

After you read this paragraph, put the book down. Find a quiet place. Settle in and contemplate these ten words—

- "You can see why God is so proud of them. . ."

I mean it!
Put the book down. Find that quiet place.
Come back only after you have contemplated what "God is so proud. . ." means.

Come back only after you have felt God's sovereign pride wrap around you.

Since you probably read this kind of paragraph and take these instructions like I do—in other words, you didn't stop, find a quiet place, or ponder the possibilities—I am going to repeat myself.

Re-read and feel the essence of this phrase—

- "You can see why God is so proud of them..."

What images and pictures do these words bring to your heart?
What feelings and emotions well up from deep, deep down in your soul?

- "You can see why God is so proud of them..."

Here is the question—

- Is it possible for God to feel this kind of pride in YOUR life?

The answer to that is an unequivocal—YES!
As a friend so clearly pointed out to me as we were talking about this concept of God's sovereign pride, God can never love you any more than the moment you believe Jesus Christ died for YOUR sins. God's love and joy and laughter and grace and presence are never so great as when you accept His free gift of eternal life. And that same amount of love and pride is what God feels for you every single moment FOR THE REST OF ETERNITY!

Even should you feel overwhelmed by your underwhelming ordinariness, the answer is—YES... God's sovereign pride is aimed at you!

Even as you see the pile of dirty laundry in the dark and lonely closets of your heart (not to mention, the very real pile of dirty clothes in the living room of your home!), the answer is—YES... God's sovereign love and grace are His gifts to you!

Even as you look back over the haunted grounds of your past, the answer is an unequivocal and absolute—YES... God yearns from the core of His being to feel this kind of sovereign pride for you!

Stop and take another minute to reflect on God's YES!

Feel God's pride... God's grace... God's love... God's sovereignty... wash over you because of His promises and His faithfulness.

Think about the way Jesus calls to us in Matthew 11—"Are you tired? Worn out? Burned out on religion?" (Matthew 11:28)

When the ordinariness of your life and the soiled burdens of your past threaten to wear you down and cause you to doubt God's sovereignty, listen to Jesus—

> Come to Me. Get away with Me and you'll recover your life. I'll show you how to take a real rest. Walk with Me and work with Me—watch how I do it. Learn the unforced rhythms of grace. I won't lay anything heavy or ill-fitting on you. Keep company with Me and you'll learn to live freely and lightly (Matthew 11:29-30).

God uses these "unforced rhythms of grace" to make us His children—

- UNFORCED in Jesus' death and resurrection.
- GRACE as He dies and lives for you.
- RHYTHMICAL as God's heartbeat becomes your heartbeat.

These same "unforced rhythms of grace" are what God sets in motion to help us live out and express our faith. Ordinary, burdened, tired, confused, and weak as we may be, God's sovereign grace brings us rest and refreshment.

Henri Nouwen was one of the most influential spiritual writers of the late 20th century. A Trappist monk, as well as, an author and professor, Henri Nouwen's greatest contributions came late in his life when he left behind a teaching position at Harvard Divinity School. Nouwen become a pastor and caregiver to "the poor in spirit." He spent his last ten years or so serving and living at a handicapped community in Toronto.

Born in Holland, but spending most of his life in the United States and Canada, in addition to following his calling as a pastor and teacher, Henri Nouwen was a lifelong lover of the circus. The acrobats and animals were special to him. But he was most fascinated with the trapeze.

At one point, Nouwen became friends with a traveling troupe of trapeze artists, "The Flying Rodleighs." He was allowed to travel with them. He attended their practice sessions. Eventually, Henri Nouwen even got to fly through the air with (not quite) the greatest of ease with them.

God's Sovereignty

As Henri Nouwen studied trapeze with "The Flying Rodleighs," he saw what he called "theology in motion." One day, the leader of the troupe, Rodleigh, made this comment about the mystery of the trapeze—"As a flyer, I must have complete trust in my catcher. The public might think that I am the great star of the trapeze, but the real star is Joe, my catcher. He has to be there for me with split-second precision and grab me out of the air as I come to him in the long jump."

This comment about the importance of the catcher caused Henri Nouwen to pause and reflect and wonder about God's grace and sovereignty.

Rodleigh continued, "The secret is that the flyer does nothing and the catcher does everything. When I fly to Joe, I have simply to stretch out my arms and hands and wait for him to catch me and pull me safely over the apron behind the catchbar."

With visions of God's sovereignty in his head, Nouwen was stopped in his thoughts—"Nothing?"

Rodleigh repeated himself, "Nothing. The worst thing the flyer can do is to try to catch the catcher. I am not supposed to catch Joe. It's Joe's task to catch me. If I grabbed Joe's wrists, I might break them, or he might break mine, and that would be the end for both of us. A flyer must fly, and a catcher must catch, and the flyer must trust, with outstretched arms, that his catcher will be there for him."[1]

Can you see images of God's faithfulness in this picture? Of God's grace? Of God's love? Of God's sovereignty? Of your relationship with God? Of faith in action?

Henri Nouwen saw the essence of God's sovereign grace and faithfulness in the trapeze—"Don't be afraid. Remember that you are the beloved child of God. He will be there when you make your long jump. Don't try to grab Him; He will grab you. Just stretch out your arms and hands and trust, trust, trust."[2]

The artistry between the flyers and the catchers of the trapeze displays the relationship between the Triune God—"The Hero of Faithfulness"—and His children.

When we allow "the Divine Catcher"—Almighty God—to catch us, we can live without fear.

When our relationship with God is based on His sovereign grace, we can put our faith into heart- and hand-felt actions of great risk.

71

When we fly as God has created us to, the conundrum of knowing Scripture and living out God's Word will be solved.

At this point, we also will be lined up with the patriarchs of Hebrews 11, hearing the inspired writer say of us—

- "You can see why God is so proud of them. . ."

Go ahead and pause again. . .
Please. . .
This time really do go and find that quiet place. . .
Reflect on the power of this statement in Hebrews 11:16. . .
Feel the grace and pride sovereignty of God wash over you. . .

- "You can see why God is so proud of them. . ."
- "You can see why God is so proud of YOU!"

While you are alone, take the words of Psalm 107 to action—

Give thanks to the Lord, for He is good; His love endures forever. Let the redeemed of the Lord say this—those He redeemed from the hand of the foe, those He gathered from the lands, from east and west, from north and south. . . Whoever is wise, let him heed these things and consider the great love of the Lord (Psalm 107:1-3, 43, NIV).

In between verse 3 and verse 43 of Psalm 107 is a litany of God's faithfulness to His gathered and redeemed children.

Over and over in the litany, the Psalmist recounts God's goodness and grace in many and various circumstances. Four times the Psalmist offers up this encouragement—"Let them give thanks to the Lord for His unfailing love and His wonderful deeds for men!" (Psalm 107:8, 15, 21, 31, NIV).

Only continue into the next chapter of this book when you have exhaled a prayer of praise and thanksgiving to the Lord God Almighty for His sovereign pride in YOU! And for His unfailing love and faithfulness to YOU!

Chapter 7

Abraham & Isaac: God's Intervention

On AETV is an award-winning reality series called *Intervention*. The premise of the show is to "profile people whose dependence on drugs and alcohol or other compulsive behavior has brought them to a point of personal crisis."[1]

In each episode, the tale is told of an individual whose life has spiraled out of control. Because of drug and alcohol abuse, life has become a seemingly endless series of tragic events. However, a loved one—be it a spouse, parent, sibling, or friend—gathers the courage and resources to stage a surprise intervention with the help of a specialist employed by the show.

The hopes of everyone involved are that the addict will respond to the intervention by recognizing how close to the brink of total personal destruction he is. If all goes according to plan, the addict will agree to enter treatment. If the script plays out properly, a once-lost life is restored to sobriety and health. According to *Intervention's* website—"The series has conducted 211 interventions since its premiere in March of 2005, 161 individuals are currently sober."[2]

At this point in our journey through Hebrews 11, the encounter between Abraham and Isaac on Mount Moriah brings the concept of intervention to the foreground. When Abraham is set to sacrifice Isaac, the entire episode hinges upon the attribute of God's intervening nature.

There is a fancy theological word that is often used when God intervenes in human events. That word is—theophany. It comes from the Greek words for "God" and "light." Literally, theophany means God-light. A theophany is an event in which God enlightens us about His nature. A theophany is a moment in real time when God interjects Himself into the course of human actions. Theophanies are God-encounters, or God-interventions, in the natural order of worldly events.

The Bible is filled with theophanies. Scripture contains numerous events in which God interjected Himself into the time and space of human history. God's Word contains many instances of God revealing Himself and His loving and gracious nature in real human lives.

The greatest theophany of all, of course, involved the 2nd Person of the Triune God, Jesus Christ. Jesus left the right hand of His Father's throne in heaven. Jesus humbled Himself and took on human flesh in Bethlehem's stable. In so doing, He became a living, breathing, ongoing theophany. For 33 years, God in Jesus Christ, walked, talked, interacted, and intervened in human history. Not only did Jesus heal, teach, lead, and guide, His ultimate purpose was to use His death and resurrection to take away the guilt and stain of all sin.

Scripture is filled with almost countless other theophanies. Small and large. Significant and seemingly insignificant. Sunday School popular and enigmatically unknown. Each theophany involves God intervening in the life of His created to take actions that enlighten us to His profound grace and generous blessing.

Think over your Bible knowledge. How many God-encounters can you list? Take a few minutes and jot some theophanies down.

- The 10 Plagues (see Exodus 7-11)
- Jericho's Wall Tumbling Down (see Joshua 6)
- The Sun Standing Still (see Joshua 10:1-15)
- Daniel in the Lion's Den (see Daniel 6)
- Peter in Prison (see Acts 12:1-18)
- Paul and the Macedonian Vision (see Acts 16:6-10)

Your list is almost guaranteed to be different than mine. Any list could go on and on.

Hebrews 11:17-19 summarizes God's theophany and intervention with Abraham and Isaac on Mount Moriah like this—

By faith, Abraham, at the time of testing, offered Isaac back to God. Acting in faith, he was as ready to return the promised son, his only son, as he had been to receive him—and this after he had already been told, 'Your descendants shall come from Isaac.' Abraham figured that if God wanted to, He could raise the dead. In a sense, that's what happened when he received Isaac back, alive from off the altar (Hebrews 11:17-19).

Think back on "the time of testing" God gave to Abraham. Following God's guidance in encounters all around the ancient Near East, Abraham and Sarah's story is found in Genesis 12-21. After more than 25 years, finally, God is faithful to keep His promise of parenthood to this couple.

"Barren Sarah" redefines the term "advanced maternal age" by conceiving a child. After a century of living, a son was born to Abraham and Sarah. After a lifetime, Abraham and Sarah had a child named Isaac, or "Laughter."

Can you imagine the sheer ecstasy, the abundance of joy and laughter that finally filled Abraham and Sarah's tent? All those decades seeing and hearing the tales of other people's children—

- "Did you hear? Little Enos rode his first camel yesterday!"
- "We are so proud of our daughter! Dinah can lace her own sandals!"
- "Great news! Zeb got accepted into rabbinical school!"
- "I just saw my sister... she is expecting another baby! This time they are saying twins!"

In a culture where womanhood was defined through motherhood, Sarah spent years feeling the shame of not having children. Abraham's shame was only slightly less because he, at least, was a successful businessman, and he did, after all, prove his virility by fathering Ishmael.

But now, after decades of feigned laughter and false joy, Abraham and Sarah finally feel the fullness of God's favor. Sarah sang—"Whoever would have suggested to Abraham that Sarah would one day nurse a baby! Yet here I am! I've given the old man a son!" (Genesis 21:7).

For this little family, life is about as good as it can get. Their tent is filled with sounds of childhood—marbles clacking, blocks being stacked, squeals of discovery, and marks of growth carved on the tent frame. Mom and Dad almost certainly dote on the boy to the point of spoiling him.

Then, sometime around the age of 12 or so, God speaks to Abraham—"Take your dear son Isaac whom you love and go to the land of Moriah. Sacrifice him there as a burnt offering on one of the mountains that I'll point out to you" (Genesis 22:2).

What?!

When I was in college taking a pre-seminary class in Hebrew, our project for the semester was to translate Genesis 22 from Hebrew into English. I was sure then, and am even more certain today, that Moses didn't get all the Holy Spirit's inspired thoughts down on his papyrus. There have to be some verses missing from the story.

Carefully read from the beginning of Genesis 22—

> After all this, God tested Abraham. God said, 'Abraham!' 'Yes?' answered Abraham. 'I'm listening.' He said, 'Take your dear son Isaac whom you love and go to the land of Moriah. Sacrifice him there as a burnt offering on one of the mountains that I'll point out to you.' Abraham got up early in the morning and saddled his donkey (Genesis 22:1-3).

There absolutely, positively has to be something missing in this narrative!

God: "Abraham! It's God! How's Isaac?"
Abraham: "Good, God."
God: "Don't say it that way, Abraham. Guess what? I've got an idea."
Abraham: "Okay, God. Are You going to tell me where I am going this time?"
God: "Very funny, Abe. Here's the plan—take Isaac, you know, your only son, Isaac, the one you and Sarah love so much. Take him over to Mount Moriah. When you get there build an altar, lay out a fire, and sacrifice him to Me."

From the fiction of my imagination, read what the Bible really does say happened next—"ABRAHAM GOT UP EARLY IN THE MORNING AND SADDLED HIS DONKEY. . ." (Genesis 22:3, emphasis added).

What?!

Where are Abraham's protests? Where is the instantaneous cessation of laughter? How about the complete and total sound of shocked silence?

The verses containing Abraham's anguish have to be languishing on a long-lost manuscript in a cave somewhere. Maybe they are buried near the great oaks at Mamre, or are lying in an urn next to Sarah's remains in the cave at Macpelah.

In God's holy and inspired Word, there are no protests or hesitations. There is only—

- A test from God.
- A faithful response from Abraham.
- A three day journey into the mountains.

Then with the place getting closer—"Abraham told his two young servants, 'Stay here with the donkey. The boy and I are going over there to worship; then we'll come back to you'" (Genesis 22:5).

Did you feel the heart of the words Abraham spoke to his servants? In what might be the most astounding statement in this entire passage, Abraham says sacrificing Isaac is going to be an act of worship!

There probably are many times (usually following lock-ins, Super Bowl parties, or retreats at summer camp!) when churches want to offer up the Junior High ministry as a sacrifice.

But, really? Sacrificing his son, his only son, whom he loves, is going to be worship?

"Acting in faith, [Abraham] was as ready to return the promised son, his only son, as he had been to receive him—and this after he had already been told, 'Your descendants shall come from Isaac'" (Hebrews 11:18).

If the passage in Hebrews 11 ended at verse 18, it might be legitimate to raise a cry about whether or not God really is "The Hero of Faithfulness."

Keep that thought in mind as the Genesis narrative continues—

"Abraham took the wood for the burnt offering and gave it to Isaac his son to carry. He carried the flint and the knife. The two of them went off together. Isaac said to Abraham his father, 'Father?' 'Yes, my son.' 'We have flint and wood, but where's the sheep for the burnt offering?' Abraham said, 'Son, God will see to it that there's a sheep for the burnt offering.' And they kept on walking together. They arrived at the place to which God had directed him (Genesis 22:6-9).

At this point, I can picture Cecil B. DeMille, fresh from directing Charlton Heston in *The Ten Commandments*, taking over the composition of Genesis 22. The events on Mount Moriah play themselves out in almost frame-by-frame, slow-motion detail—

- Abraham takes the wood off Isaac's shoulders. (Picture Isaac stretching and flexing his muscles.)
- Abraham builds an altar. (Pan the mountainside and zero in on the altar.)
- He lays out the wood. (Picture father and son standing side-by-side admiring the altar and woodpile.)
- He ties up Isaac. (Cut to confused look on Isaac's face.)
- He lays Isaac on the altar. (Close up on Isaac's face.)
- Abraham reaches out his arm. (Shift to Abraham's face.)
- He takes the knife from his scabbard. (Hear the sound of the metal blade rasping against the leather scabbard.)
- He raises the knife over his head. (Cue the dramatic music.)
- He has the knife ready to move down to the boy's throat. (Crescendo the music.)
- Abraham is about to kill Isaac. (Silence... and... freeze-frame.)

"Just then an angel of God called to him out of Heaven, 'Abraham! Abraham!' 'Yes, I'm listening.' 'Don't lay a hand on that boy! Don't touch him! Now I know how fearlessly you fear God; you didn't hesitate to place your son, your dear son, on the altar for Me'" (Genesis 22:11-12).

Theophany!
At exactly the right moment, God intervened.
Just as Abraham was about to slash the knife across Isaac's throat, God made His presence in the altar area known.

"Abraham looked up. He saw a ram caught by its horns in the thicket. Abraham took the ram and sacrificed it as a burnt offering instead of his son" (Genesis 22:13).

In case you (unfortunately!) think like me, that there had to be something missing back between verses 2 and 3, did you catch what God said in His intervention and comments to Abraham in verse 12?

"Don't lay a hand on that boy! Don't touch him! Now I know how fearlessly you fear God; you DIDN'T HESITATE to place your son, your dear son, on the altar for Me" (Genesis 22:12, emphasis added).

God spoke. Abraham listened.
God commanded. Abraham acted—WITHOUT HESITATION.
Abraham journeyed, prepared, and offered.
God never stopped watching.
God never ceased being with Abraham and Isaac.
God was always ready to intervene at exactly the right moment.

Abraham's faith is summed up in Hebrews 11:19—"Abraham figured that if God wanted to, He could raise the dead. In a sense, that's what happened when he received Isaac back, alive from off the altar" (Hebrews 11:19).

Some years ago, Amy Grant had a hit song called *Angels*. The lyrics include these—

> God only knows the times
> My life was threatened just today
> A reckless car ran out of gas
> Before it ran my way
> Near misses all around me
> Accidents unknown
> Though I never see with human eyes
> The hands that lead me home
> But I know they're all around me
> All day and through the night
> When the enemy is closing in
> I know sometimes they fight
> To keep my feet from falling

I'll never turn away
If you're asking what's protecting me
Then you're gonna hear me say
Got His angels watching over me, every move I make
Angels watching over me
Angels watching over me, every step I take
Angels watching over me[3]

This song describes the essence of theophany. God's divine attribute of an ongoing, ever-present, intervening nature. He lives to intervene in our lives. God exists for close encounters of the intervention kind with you and me!

"Though I never see with human eyes The hands that lead me home. . ." God is present and God is always ready to intervene at exactly the right moment in your life and mine.

Whatever your test from God is, two things are certain—

- God will never allow you to be tested beyond your capacity.
- God is ready at all times to intervene on your behalf.

Your current test may be found in a highly-charged and emotionally volatile situation like the one faced by Abraham and Isaac on Mount Moriah.

Or God may intervene in your life in countless ways you are never aware of—like the proverbial "reckless truck that ran out of gas" before it ran your way.

Regardless, know these divine facts—

- God is real.
- God is present.
- God is watching.
- And, God is ready to intervene for you.

With that said—

- Are you ready for your God-encounters today?

Chapter 8

Isaac: God's Heritage

*A*braham binds Isaac securely to a woodpile. He raises a knife over the boy's head to kill him. And, with perfect timing, God intervenes telling Abraham, "Don't lay a hand on the boy."

Instead, Abraham sacrificed a ram caught in a nearby bush.

Interestingly, getting tied up by his father in Genesis 22:10, was the last time Isaac was mentioned by name. Although the Bible doesn't specifically tell us so, Isaac must have been freed from bondage on that woodpile altar.

We are told after God provided the ram for the sacrifice that— "Abraham went back to his young servants. They got things together and returned to Beersheba. Abraham settled down in Beersheba" (Genesis 22:19).

Abraham goes home from the scene of sacrifice on Mount Moriah. Abraham returns to Beersheba where God continues to favor and bless him. Even the servants who were left at the base of the mount, we are told, return to Beersheba with Abraham.

But what about Isaac?

What happened to Isaac after his father tied him up and was ready to kill him?

Where did Isaac go from Mount Moriah?

Maybe, most important of all, what were the effects Isaac took with him from this experience?

I can't recall ever reading or hearing about what psychological traumas Isaac may have suffered on Mount Moriah. There had to be some emotional scarring—a teenage boy taken on a three-day journey deep into the mountains, bound and laid on a sacrificial altar, held there at knifepoint... and all by his father... who supposedly loved him!

Talk about PTSAD!

Talk about a serious case of "Post-Traumatic Sacrificial Altar Disorder"! If ever a psychological complex or syndrome was crying out to be identified this has to be it!

However, the Bible provides no details about Isaac's after-effects from this harrowing experience. As a matter of fact, the next time Isaac is mentioned by name, it is some years later. In Genesis 24, Abraham sends a servant back to the homeland to secure a wife for "the boy."

Isaac's bout with PTSAD could have two—not mutually exclusive—results. As he reflected back on that day, he could have recalled a powerful example of his father following God's will so completely. Isaac could have felt deep down in his being what Hebrews 11 declares about Abraham's faith—"Abraham reasoned that God could raise the dead, and figuratively speaking, he did receive Isaac back from death" (Hebrews 11:19, NIV).

AND—not OR—AND... Isaac could have felt some scars from what had to have been a hugely traumatic event for a 13-year-old boy to undergo.

Instead of any details on Isaac's recall of the events on Mount Moriah, he unassumingly recedes into Scripture's background. Only when we read Hebrews 11:20 does Isaac step from the shadows. With a rather brief and vague statement, we read—"By an act of faith, Isaac reached into the future as he blessed Jacob and Esau" (Hebrews 11:20).

Reading about Isaac in the last chapter raises a question about Isaac's life—did the trauma of Mount Moriah affect the way Isaac parented his own sons, Jacob and Esau?

We are told Esau was a redneck man's man—a hunter and gatherer extraordinaire. Esau was hairy and sweaty. He could probably grunt on par with the star of the 90s sitcom *Home Improvement*, "Tim 'The Toolman' Taylor." Odds are Esau was the inventor of man caves and duct tape.

Jacob—not so much. Jacob, at the other extreme, was a momma's boy. Jacob was soft, delicate, and sweet-smelling. (Not quite "The Toolman's" sidekick, Al Borland, but you get the flannel-flavored picture.)

What role did Isaac's experience at Abraham's knifepoint play in the upbringing and lives of these twin boys?

In many ways, we are each a composite of all the events of our past. Good or bad. Remembered or forgotten. Important or insignificant. Helpful or hurt-filled. All the interactions of our past—whether this morning on the way to work, or forever and two days ago—have combined to make us the person we are today.

In the movie *Cars II*, the lovable, redneck tow truck, Tow Mater, has the opportunity to get his dents fixed and repaired. He turns down the chance to get a classic, full body makeover because each rust-filled dent marks a story from his past. Every scratch and ding on his beat-up frame is a reminder to Mater of an adventure he shared with his best friend, Lightning McQueen.

Christ-follower and Christian thinker Leonard Sweet captures the essence of our scars perfectly—

> [Christ-followers] don't need to hide their perfect scars and imperfections. We can let our flaws hang out and let our hair down, and we will find that we are trusted more for our vulnerability than for our virtues. In fact, our scars can be stigmata of divine power and blessing.[1]

Our scars and wounds contain important stories from our past that have shaped us into the person we are right now.

Literally—

- The scars on my right shin bring smiles and memories from good times playing goalkeeper on my college soccer team.
- The scar on my right wrist brings a few less smiles as I remember the afternoon I dropped a friend's refrigerator while helping him move from one apartment to another.

And, figuratively—

- The internal scars I carry from my Dad's death.
- The emotional marks left from the miscarriage my wife suffered.

- The spiritual wounds inflicted on me and my family by fellow Christians.

Whether literal or figurative, my scars and traumas have made me who I am today.

Likewise, your scars have made you—you.

The question is—

- Will we learn to appreciate our dents and scratches like Tow Mater?
- Or will our scars debilitate us and cause us no end of grief today and tomorrow?

As we consider Isaac, and the scars he had to have carried away from Mount Moriah, one of the most critical understanding about scars is that they are not—by definition—negative. Normally, we hear the word "scar" and we think something bad happened. However, many scars—while reminders of painful events—are really blessings.

For example, I have two more scars on my right shoulder from surgery to repair a torn labrum (suffered while playing goalkeeper on that college soccer team). I lived with the tear for almost twenty years until having surgery a few years ago. I also have matching scars on my palms and wrists from two carpal tunnel surgeries. Without these scars and the repairs to my arm and hands that they facilitated, I would not have been able to take part-time jobs washing windows or painting while writing this book. (Every author needs to do something to pay the bills while writing his first book!)

Likewise, the scars on my palms are reminders of the conversations about Jesus' resurrection I had with my surgeon—during my surgery! (Talk about an interesting *Ebenezer*!)

It is critical to see your scars as part of God's plan FOR you and as part of who God has made you TO BE!

Hebrews 11 puts this insight into evidence with its words about Isaac—"By an act of faith, Isaac reached into the future as he blessed Jacob and Esau" (Hebrews 11:20).

The only way Isaac could "reach into the future" was by not dwelling on the negative aspects of the scars inflicted by his traumatic past. The only way Isaac could bless Esau and Jacob was by stepping forward from the trauma in faith. The only way Isaac could pass a Godly heritage to his boys was by trusting that the events of his past were under God's guidance and control.

Perhaps as a symbol of his ability to overcome the past, as Isaac's years were exacting their toll on him, his eyesight begins to fail him. From a state near blindness, he realizes his days are drawing to a close. Isaac wants to pass along a family blessing to his firstborn son, Esau.

Instead, smooth-skinned, sweet-smelling Jacob (with the prodding, plotting, and conniving of his mother, Rebekah, egging him on) dresses up like hairy, sweaty, earthy-smelling Esau.

With a bowl of stew, Jacob tricks blind Isaac into giving him the family blessing—

> "May God give you of Heaven's dew and Earth's bounty of grain and wine. May peoples serve you and nations honor you. You will master your brothers, and your mother's sons will honor you. Those who curse you will be cursed, those who bless you will be blessed." And then right after Isaac had blessed Jacob and Jacob had left, Esau showed up from the hunt (Genesis 27:28-30).

Add yet more scars—and opportunities to grow past their pain—to Isaac's lifetime collection.

- A lifetime ago, his father—in a monumental display of faith—had tried to kill him.
- Now, his son steals the family blessing (after having already swindled Esau out of the first-born's birthright).
- And, his wife is the master chef behind all the trickery and thievery.

Talk about traumatic! Talk about opportunity for God to prove the promise He would later give through Saint Paul in Romans 8:28— "And we know that in all things God works for the good of those who love Him, who have been called according to His purpose" (Romans 8:28, NIV).

After everything that has happened in his life, including this most recent trauma, Isaac still reaches for the future. From behind his little-seeing eyes, Isaac wants Jacob to go back to the land of his family's heritage to find a wife.

Amazingly—and grace-filledly (forget about Spell-Check. . . "grace-filledly" is a word!), Isaac sends his conniving, thieving, second-born son off with a second blessing—"May The Strong God bless you and give you many, many children, a congregation of peoples; and pass on the blessing of Abraham to you and your descendants so that you will get this land in which you live, this land God gave Abraham" (Genesis 28:3-4).

How was Isaac able to voluntarily—even, eagerly—bless Jacob a second time after everything Jacob had stolen from him?

How was Isaac able to grow past the pain inflicted by the scars of his past (both the fading scars of his far, distant past, and the bright pink, fresh scars of his immediate, recent past) behind to pass a Godly heritage into his family's future?

How about you?

How about me?

How can we grow through the pain of our scars and traumas so as to reach into the future to pay a Godly heritage forward to our children and grandchildren?

Quite possibly the only way for us to pass along a Godly heritage is to follow Isaac's example. This may sound trite, but it is far from so. Isaac is only able to pass a Godly heritage "into the future" because of grace. Without God's grace in his life, Isaac most probably would have become a blind, bitter, old man brought low by the accumulated baggage of his past.

Instead, Isaac "reaches into the future" of his children and grand-children's lives with grace. Isaac reaches forward with the grace of "The Hero of Faithfulness." Isaac passes along such Godly blessings to his descendants who will comprise the future generations by the sole power of the grace of the Strong God of Adam and Noah and Abraham.

From the midst of their own scars and traumas, the Puritan followers of Jesus Christ of the 16th and 17th centuries were able to maintain perspective on Godly grace and blessings, as well. One Puritan

Prayer captures the grace of God that helps us overcome our scars and pass forward blessings into our future—

> O bottomless Fountain of all good, I am astonished at the difference. . . between my receivings—and my deservings, between the state I am now in—and my past gracelessness, between the heaven I am bound for—and the hell I merit. Who made me to differ, but You? I could not have begun to love You, had You not first loved me. Lord, I am astonished that. . . such a crown should fit the head of such a sinner! such high advancement be for an unfruitful person! such joys for so vile a rebel! Let 'wrath deserved' be written on the door of hell, but the 'free gift of grace' on the gate of heaven! Let Your love draw me nearer to Yourself. Wean me from sin, mortify me to this world, and make me ready for my departure hence. Secure me by Your grace as I sail across this stormy sea.[2]

Having just read these words, stop!
Pause.
Re-read them.
Pause.
Dwell for as long as necessary on these three words—"I am astonished. . ."
Now. . . stop. . . and consider this question—

- What astonishes you about God?

This Puritan prayer-poem hinges on two concepts—"receivings" and "deservings." "Receiving" from God what He gives by grace and "deserving" from God what we earn by our sin.

Thinking about your "receivings" and your "deservings," how would you compare them?

- What have you "received" from God?
- What have you "deserved" from God?

As you continue to pause and ponder and pray, try to plumb the depths of these three words again—"I am astonished. . ."

- Any new insights into what astonishes you about God?

How about—

- That the crown of eternal life fits perfectly on your sinful head. . .
- That in spite of your lack of faithfulness, God advances you by grace into His family. . .
- That God overflows joy into your life, even given your rebellion (and the resulting pain, and yes, scars) against Him. . .

Try on these questions again—

- What are my "deservings"?
- What are my "receivings"?

One more time—

- What astonishes you about "The Hero of Faithfulness"?

Only when he was able to differentiate between his "deservings" and his "receivings" could Isaac "reach into the future" to pass along a Godly heritage and blessing to Jacob.

As you wrestle with your scars and your traumas—and the results of those scar-inducing traumas—read carefully these words from King Solomon in Proverbs 1. Keep in mind your "deservings" and your "receivings"—

> These are the wise sayings of Solomon. . . Written down so we'll know how to live well and right, to understand what life means and where it's going. . . To teach the inexperienced the ropes and give our young people a grasp on reality. . . Fresh wisdom to probe and penetrate, the rhymes and reasons of wise men and women. Start with God—the first step in

learning is bowing down to God; only fools thumb their noses at such wisdom and learning (Proverbs 1:1-7).

In order to "grasp reality" and learn from (not be bound, conflicted, and constrained by) the past, wise King Solomon gives this advice—"Start with God!" (Proverbs 1:7).

Other translations say—"The fear of the Lord is the beginning of knowledge, but fools despise wisdom and discipline" (Proverbs 1:7, NIV).

The beginning (the middle, the end, and everywhere else in between, also!) of wisdom for Isaac came as he saw his father Abraham's knife-point example of complete faith in God's call. Only by starting with God, and receiving grace from "The Hero of Faithfulness," could Isaac "reach into the future and bless Jacob and Esau."

After Jacob stole the family blessing from Isaac, the intended recipient, first-born Esau brought his pot of homemade stew to Isaac. When Esau found out what Jacob (and his mother) had done, he was inconsolable. Esau begged his father for any crumb of a blessing that might be leftover. So, as Hebrews 11 says, Isaac blessed Esau, just as he had Jacob.

Contemplate Esau's blessing—"You'll live far from Earth's bounty, remote from Heaven's dew. You'll live by your sword, hand-to-mouth, and you'll serve your brother. But when you can't take it any more you'll break loose and run free" (Genesis 27:39-40).

Not so sweet sounding. Esau's blessing sounds more like graphic tragedy than Godly blessing. Esau certainly acquired his own scars from these words. He also spent a lifetime angry and bitter over Jacob's treachery. Esau's blessing sounds harsh, that is, until we read the last two phrases carefully—"But when you can't take it any more you'll break loose and run free" (Genesis 27:40b).

In other words, Esau's life will be marked by pain and scars and trauma. However, there will always be hope on his horizon. At some point, Esau will have had spent enough energy on anger and desire for retribution against Jacob. At some future time, Esau will have the opportunity to compare his "deservings" and his "receivings." Eventually, Esau will see God's provision in ALL the happenings of his past and he will come out from beneath the burden of anger and vengeance.

Eventually, the two brothers reunited in Genesis 33 under these conditions—

> Esau looked around and saw the women and children: 'And who are these with you?' Jacob said, 'The children that God saw fit to bless me with.' Then the maidservants came up with their children and bowed; then Leah and her children, also bowing; and finally, Joseph and Rachel came up and bowed to Esau. Esau then asked, 'And what was the meaning of all those herds that I met?' 'I was hoping that they would pave the way for my master to welcome me.' Esau said, 'Oh, brother. I have plenty of everything—keep what is yours for yourself.' Jacob said, 'Please. If you can find it in your heart to welcome me, accept these gifts. When I saw your face, it was as the face of God smiling on me. Accept the gifts I have brought for you. God has been good to me and I have more than enough.' Jacob urged the gifts on him and Esau accepted. Then Esau said, 'Let's start out on our way; I'll take the lead' (Genesis 33:5-12).

Isaac's blind eyes saw the way to future blessing of Esau and Jacob.

Esau broke loose from his own scars and ran free into a relationship with Jacob.

Even Jacob recovered from his deceit and trickery to become the third in the designation—"The God of Abraham, Isaac, and Jacob."

Now, what about you?

Are you ready to take stock of your "receivings" and your "deservings"?

Are you ready to break down your scar tissue and run free from the pain of your past's traumas?

If so, know the truth—God is faithful! God is ready! God is able! God's heritage is to bless and preserve you! God's desire is lead you to complete joy and peace!

If you are ready to run free from your scars—"Start with God—the first step in learning is bowing down to God!" (Proverbs 1:7).

Chapter 9

Jacob: God's Blessings

"Welcome to my hometown of Lake Wobegon..." Hearing these eagerly anticipated words, the audience bursts into applause and cheers and whistles. Another monologue from humorist and satirist Garrison Keillor is off and wandering through the streets and homes and, most insightfully, the lives of the people in the fictional Minnesota burg of Lake Wobegon.

For over forty years, countless people from around the world have been taking weekly journeys to "the little town that time forgot, and the decades cannot improve... [the town] where all the women are strong, all the men are good-looking, and all the children are above average."[1]

With wisdom, humor, and insight few possess, Garrison Keillor has created a fictional world that caricatures all-too-closely the human frailties of our own world. Through the wonder of Keillor's storytelling, the timeless folk of Lake Wobegon also help us catch ongoing glimpses of the details, the quantity, and the simplicity of God's blessings in our lives today.

In Hebrews 11:21, the concept of blessings and, more specifically, the act of passing blessings along from one person to another becomes central. As we follow the Scriptures to Jacob's bedside, he is found giving a blessing to Joseph's two sons—"By an act of faith, Jacob on his deathbed blessed each of Joseph's sons in turn, blessing them with God's blessing, not his own—as he bowed worshipfully upon his staff" (Hebrews 11:21).

In Genesis 49, Jacob gives blessings to Reuben, Simeon, Judah, and all his other sons. However, Hebrews 11 only makes reference to Jacob's faith—and God's faithfulness—in the blessings given to Joseph's two sons, Manasseh and Ephraim, in Genesis 48.

Following his heart-rending and heart-stopping reunion with Joseph, Jacob relocated seventy members of his family from drought-stricken Canaan to the lush pastures and meadows of Goshen, in Egypt. Once settled, Jacob lived another seventeen years (see Genesis 47:28).

Eventually, age and illness began to overtake Jacob. From his offices in the Egyptian centers of power, Joseph received word of his father's failing health. He left his labors as the nation's second-in-command and traveled to Goshen, so he could pay a visit to his dying father.

As I am working on the early drafts of this chapter, my 95-year-old Grandma Ada is in the hospital in Indiana. My Mom and aunts and uncles are talking about visiting their mother from their various corners of the country (literally, from Maine to California). Each email and phone conversation is tinged with a bit of "this-might-be-it."

- Is it time for all five children to gather?
- Should the grandkids and great-grandkids be checking flight schedules on the travel websites?

With equivalent thoughts given to chariot schedules and camel caravans, Joseph made the journey across Egypt to his father's bedside in Goshen. Because of the distances involved and the seriousness of Jacob's illness, Joseph also brought his two sons to visit their grandpa one more time.

As the visit unfolded, the ailing Jacob was delighted to spend time with his long-lost and most-favored son, Joseph. Jacob also took delight in being with the two grandsons he never knew he had.

As the visit wound down, Joseph's two sons, Manasseh and Ephraim, took their places before their grandfather. With some solemnity, the young men stood still as Grandpa Jacob slowly got out of his bed to bless them.

In a subtle switch (almost reminiscent of the nuanced relationships explored in a Garrison Keillor monologue), when Jacob leaned on his cane so he could bless his grandsons, he "crossed his arms and put his right hand on the head of Ephraim who was the younger and his left hand on the head of Manasseh, the firstborn. Then he blessed them" (Genesis 48:16).

Joseph, reacting like a properly-concerned, overly-attentive, hovering-nearby, helicopter-parent, moves quickly to address his ailing father's mistake—"[Joseph] took hold of his father's hand to move it from Ephraim's head to Manasseh's, saying, 'That's the wrong head, Father; the other one is the firstborn; place your right hand on his head'" (Genesis 48:18).

Sensing he might only have a few decisions remaining before he dies, Jacob was not about to endure any correction from Joseph—"'I know, my son; but I know what I'm doing. He [Manasseh, the elder brother] also will develop into a people, and he also will be great. But his younger brother [Ephraim] will be even greater and his descendants will enrich nations.' Then he blessed them both. . ." (Genesis 48:19-20).

Some thirty-five or so centuries later, our culture is very different. Beyond characters like George Clooney's in the movie *O Brother, Where Art Thou*, the laws of primogeniture and the rights of the *pater familias* are hardly mentioned, let alone applied. I believe—as a firstborn son of two firstborn parents, married to a firstborn daughter of two firstborn parents—the laws of primogeniture and the rights of the *pater familias* should count for something!

Still and all, this hand-switching thing Jacob pulls with his grandsons doesn't seem like a very big deal.

- Manasseh and Ephraim. . .
- Ephraim and Manasseh. . .
- Older and younger. . .
- Younger and older. . .

Too often, we read the Bible as if everyone in it was some kind of both spiritual and physical superhero. This is a real problem for us because the Bible is filled with "regular" people. From Adam to today, only sinful, struggling, "regular" people have ever inhabited this world.

You know, the kind of "regular" people I'm talking about. The kind of regular people who live on the same city blocks we live on.

The kind of struggling people who walk with limps and who possess secrets as in the fictional Lake Wobegon. The kind of sinful people who could almost turn the scene at Jacob's bedside into an Abbot and Costello routine—

- "Who's on the left?"
- "Manasseh's on the right."
- "What's on the right?"
- "Ephraim's on the left."
- "I don't know is on which side?"
- "What's that in your hair?"
- "You have something stuck in your teeth."

Joseph spent at least three decades separated from his family, living and ruling in the formality of the royal Egyptian courts. In Genesis 48, he was probably feeling the emotional weight of what could be his last visit with his father. Understandably, he wants everything to be exactly proper.

Jacob, after 147 years of life (years that included a couple long, lonely decades believing his favorite son, Joseph, was dead), couldn't care less about formality. He knows exactly what he is doing.

The entire process reminds me of a favorite Garrison Keillor quote—"God writes a lot of comedy... the trouble is, He's stuck with so many bad actors who don't know how to play funny."[2]

Instead of being like prim and proper Joseph, trying to arrange God's hand perfectly in our lives, perhaps we could look for God's comedy and "play funny" in life's ordinary events a bit more frequently. If we each took a little starch out of our stiff-necked and serious lives, we might notice the humor God has placed all around us. I would go so far as to bet, if we laughed at our foibles and frailties fractionally more frequently, the cholesterol, blood pressure, and antidepressant medication markets might just collapse!

Returning to Jacob's crossed-arm blessing to Ephraim and Manasseh, God's writing into human history brings the handing of blessing from one person to another to the center of our attention. Take a glance at some of the traditional ways this verse is cast—

- King James Version—"By faith Jacob, when he was a dying, blessed both the sons of Joseph; and worshipped, leaning upon the top of his staff."
- New International Version—"By faith Jacob, when he was dying, blessed each of Joseph's sons, and worshiped as he leaned on the top of his staff."
- New American Standard (italics in original) —"By faith Jacob, as he was dying, blessed each of the sons of Joseph, and worshiped, *leaning* on the top of his staff."
- New Living Translation—"It was by faith that Jacob, when he was old and dying, blessed each of Joseph's sons and bowed in worship as he leaned on his staff."
- The Amplified Version (brackets in original) —"[Prompted] by faith Jacob, when he was dying, blessed each of Joseph's sons and bowed in prayer over the top of his staff."
- English Standard Version—"By faith Jacob, when dying, blessed each of the sons of Joseph, bowing in worship over the head of his staff."

Essentially, all the translations and versions are the same—

- Dying Jacob, blessed his grandsons, and worshiped or prayed over them.

Now look closely at *The Message's* rendering of Hebrews 11:21—

- "By an act of faith, Jacob on his deathbed blessed each of Joseph's sons in turn, blessing them with God's blessing, not his own—as he bowed worshipfully upon his staff."

Did you notice the extra bit of phrasing *The Message* provides in these words?

Here is the specific phrase from Hebrews 11:21, in *The Message*, to study again—

- ". . . blessing them with God's blessing, not his own. . ."

The added insight is this—the blessings provided by Jacob to Ephraim and Manasseh are not just token gifts grandpa passed along to his grandsons. Jacob is not just giving Ephraim his favorite walking stick and Manasseh his butterfly collection.

The blessings Jacob is handing down to Ephraim and Manasseh are special reminders of divine favor and faithfulness. Most important, these blessings are not Jacob's own. These are God's blessings being given by God through Grandpa Jacob to grandsons Ephraim and Manasseh.

Is Eugene Peterson taking liberties with the original language?

Or is he illuminating a subtle, yet powerful, reminder to us?

Here is what I want you to do—

- Take a moment...
- Pause...
- Consider what this added phrase is really saying...

Are you situated?

Read the phrase again—

- "... blessing them with God's blessing, not his own..."

How powerful is that?

Set aside for a moment the startling prophetic content of the blessing—that the Egyptian-born sons of Joseph (and his Egyptian wife), Ephraim and Manasseh, are going to be remembered as nations as great as the divinely chosen line of Hebrew patriarchs—Abraham, Isaac, and Jacob.

Take a deep breath and center your thoughts and emotions solely on the concept of blessings. Specifically—

- "... blessing them with God's blessing, not his own..."

What if every time we uttered the words—

- "Blessings..."
- "Bless you..."

- "God bless. . ."
- "God bless you. . ."

What if our hearts and souls rose from the depths of our spiritual laziness to follow Jacob's worshipful posture?

What if we truly prayed these "blessings" upon others like we were passing along God's greatest riches and most personal desires to the person we were engaging?

Instead of a throw-away line tossed out like a Kleenex after a sneeze—"Bless you."

Rather than a rote sign-off to "Christian-ize" our correspondence—"God bless you."

What if we "bowed worshipfully" and spoke prayerfully our "blessings"?

What differences might a soul-felt prayer for God to deeply and powerfully impart the fullness of His divine blessing to the person we were addressing make?

What kinds of subtle shifts and not-so-slight impacts could such prayers, such blessing others with God's blessings, have on us and the people and culture around us?

If we "play funny" just a bit more and, in so doing, shift some of the pharmaceutical markets, imagine what could happen if we prayed—seriously and consciously. . . powerfully and regularly—the radicalness of God's blessings onto each person we encounter!

While you consider the potentially powerful spiritual dynamics of these shifts, allow these words from 2 Peter 1 to filter through your thoughts. Focus on the adjectives and feel the flow of God's blessing through them. As he greets his audience in his Second Letter, Peter says—

> So don't lose a minute in building on what you've been given, complementing your basic faith with good character, spiritual understanding, alert discipline, passionate patience, reverent wonder, warm friendliness, and generous love, each dimension fitting into and developing the others. With these qualities active and growing in your lives, no grass will grow under your

feet, no day will pass without its reward as you mature in your experience of our Master Jesus (2 Peter 1:5-8).

Just as I was writing these paragraphs at my favorite table in my favorite coffee shop, God blessed (?) me with an intrusive conversation.

Of course, as the parenthetical "question mark" implies, I didn't originally believe this to be the case. I was deep in thought. My brow was furrowed. My pen was flashing across my pages of my yellow legal pad. My ink was flowing and my words were pouring out of me with fury and fascination.

Then, all of a sudden, a writer's nightmare. I looked up, flexed my fingers to offset a cramp, and the gentleman at the next table in the coffee shop asked what I was working on.

Egads!

As I tried not to display my irritation, or lose my train of thought, I began describing this book on God's attributes being displayed in Hebrews 11. What began an intrusion, quickly became a great conversation on what Christians could do to have more positive influence on society today.

The heart of my coffee-shop compatriot's argument (as a person who described himself as not "currently" a Christian) could have been straight from 2 Peter. In so many words, what would impress him in Christian behavior?

- Good character
- Spiritual understanding
- Alert discipline
- Passionate patience
- Reverent wonder
- Warm friendliness
- Generous love

In spite of my irritation at being interrupted, "The Hero of Faithfulness" was at work. God was the One interrupting so He could give me a blessing.

The blessing?

What if we prayed for these specific "2 Peter 1" blessings to be imparted to others each time we told someone—"God bless you"?

And I don't mean just the attributes Peter lists. What if we prayed for these specific intensifying adjectives that accompany the attributes to be imparted to those for whom we pray?

What if we prayed for God to faithfully bestow—

- GOOD character
- PASSIONATE patience
- REVERENT wonder
- GENEROUS love

What if our relationship with "The Hero of Faithfulness" caused us to be used by Him more frequently as a means to blessing others?

What if the work of the Holy Spirit in our relationships led us to bow worshipfully and pray intensely for these divine attributes to be imparted to others each time we said—"God bless you!"

Before you go on to read the next chapter, here is a suggestion—

Take a walk around the block...

Go to that special place of yours...

Take some time to pray and seek God's blessing...

Ask God to faithfully work through you just as He blessed Ephraim and Manasseh through their Grandfather Jacob.

Ask God to faithfully increase His blessings to others through your "bless you's"—and to do so in great and mighty ways that bring Him glory and others hope.

Ask God to faithfully grant you His Holy Spirit to help you pray for intensive, personal, powerful adjectives to accompany His blessing to those you pray for.

While you take that walk and say those prayers, I'll try to figure out why I ended my conversation in the coffee shop with a handshake and a really, really lame—"Take care..."

Instead of a passionate, prayerful, and generous—"God bless you!"

Chapter 10

Joseph: God's Dreams

The boys looked sharp. Their freshly laundered Wood River All-Stars jerseys were forest green, with black numbers, outlined in white. The uniform was capped off by gray baseball pants and a matching green hat bearing a black-on-white "WR". With nervous chatter filling the dugout, these boys were ready to play baseball.

Their opponents also looked good in white baseball pants, with royal blue jerseys, highlighted by red numbers and white trim. The ball field was covered with luscious green grass. The infield sported freshly manicured red-dirt. The white chalk batter's boxes and baselines were thick and bright.

Players and families from both teams had gathered early on a late June Saturday morning, at the Sawtooth Baseball Fields, in Twin Falls, Idaho, for the elimination rounds of the 9-10 year-old Cal Ripken All-Star Tournament.

While the opposing pitcher finished his warm-up tosses, Jon-Jon was loosening up in the on-deck circle. Just as the umpire shouted baseball's magic words—"Play Ball!"—his dad leaned forward on the bleachers and said through the fence, "Jon-Jon! Smile! You are livin' the dream!"

Laughing, smiling, and popping another handful of cracked pepper sunflower seeds into my mouth, I echoed the sentiment, "Man, you've got that right."

All-too-often these days, far-too-many people forget the dream-lives we are living. Especially in the United States of America, our lives are positively dreamy. More often than not, however, it seems, we either complain about how we are living, or we dream about living alltogether differently. Rarely, it seems, do we look around and realize the dream lives God has given us to live.

Hebrews 11:22 sets our attention on Joseph's faith—and on God's faithfulness to him—in this succinct statement—"By an act of faith, Joseph, while dying, prophesied the exodus of Israel, and made arrangements for his own burial" (Hebrews 11:22).

Even the quickest glance through Joseph's life reveals the high occurrence of dreams and dream interpretations. From dreams of sun, moon, and stars as a youth, to a baker's and cupbearer's dreams in prison, to Pharaoh's dreams of fat and skinny cattle, dreams played a significant role across most of Joseph's 110 years.

Whenever he was faced with an interesting set of dreams, the choice Joseph dealt with was whether or not he would live out the messages conveyed in the dreams, or just file the dreams away and, instead, dream about living.

Hebrews 11 establishes Joseph's faith—and gives us insight into his choice—by drawing on the final verses of Genesis 50—

> At the end, Joseph said to his brothers, 'I am ready to die. God will most certainly pay you a visit and take you out of this land and back to the land he so solemnly promised to Abraham, Isaac, and Jacob.' Then Joseph made the sons of Israel promise under oath, 'When God makes His visitation, make sure you take my bones with you as you leave here.' Joseph died at the age of 110 years. They embalmed him and placed him in a coffin in Egypt (Genesis 50:24-26).

From the beginning to the end of Joseph's life, here is a quick thumbnail sketch of the highlights—

- 1st-born son of Jacob's favorite wife and true love, Rachel
- Jacob's 11th-born son when all his wives and handmaids are counted
- Most favored son of all Jacob's children

- Despised by his older brothers for bragging about his dreams and for strutting around in his coat-of-many-colors
- Sold into slavery by the same jealous and angry older brothers who told their father, Jacob, Joseph had been mauled by wild animals
- Bought from slave traders by a prominent Egyptian leader, in whose home he rose in responsibility
- Imprisoned on false rape charges
- Interpreted dreams in prison and rose in authority
- Released from prison after interpreting Pharaoh's dream about impending feast and famine years
- Appointed 2nd-in-command of Egypt so he could oversee Egypt's famine survival system
- Toyed with his brothers when they came from Canaan to Egypt for food
- Reunited with his father and family
- Died in Egypt with the promise of being reburied in the Promised Land

From the pit to the penthouse, Joseph's last words in Genesis 50 couldn't be more accurate in summing up both his life and God's faithfulness—"God WILL DO as HE pleases" (Genesis 50:24, emphasis added).

Let's set aside any starry-eyed, dreamy thoughts.

Let's stop and become brutally honest for a minute—

- If anyone had reason to be stuck in the rut of dreaming about living, it should have been Joseph.

Answer me this—who is thrown into a pit and left to die, only to be removed from the pit and sold into slavery. Then, whose life follows slavery with false imprisonment for several years, all while being separated from family for many decades. Yet who comes through it all both with a dream life and with the ability to live out the dream life?

Are you kidding me?

No one. There is not a single person who can accomplish that on his or her own human strength.

If, however, we factor God's strength and grace and power into the equation, then the potential exists for everyone—from Joseph to any of his brothers. . . to all of you, as well as, to me—to both experience and live out an absolute dream-life.

Joseph's life—from the pit of despair, to the prison of loneliness, to the pinnacle of Egyptian power—highlights one of God's greatest attributes. Joseph's life reveals that God dreams big dreams. And God's dreams for His children are not limited by our diminished scope or paltry scale.

At the core of God's ways of working in our world are God's big, hairy, and audacious dreams for every single one of His children. God's dreams are so significant that to live them out in our lives would revolutionize not just our own lives, but the entire world.

There is, however, a downside to these God-sized dreams. The lousy part of God's dreams? Most of us miss out on God's dreams, because we are afraid to seize His grace and live out His plans for our lives.

Think about the supreme creativity of God's dreams for Joseph's life. If you or I were going to make an international statesman out of Joseph, none of us would have come up with a script that included ten angry brothers, an Ishmaelite caravan, the dreams of an imprisoned baker and cupbearer (we may have had one or the other, but both?), or a seven-year feast followed by a seven-year famine. We certainly would not have been creative enough to culminate everything in a Walton's mountain-style family reunion—complete with heaping helpings of mashed potatoes and dining room hospitality.

Even from a company called "Dreamworks," Steven Spielberg, Jeffrey Katzenberg, and David Geffen couldn't have come up with this script.

None of us could have designed Joseph's dream life.

But God can. . . and He did!

Which highlights the point God made through the prophet Isaiah, in Isaiah 55:8—"'For My thoughts are not your thoughts, neither are your ways My ways,' declares the Lord" (Isaiah 55:8, NIV).

Wrestling through the implications of God's dreams being different (and, in this case, "different" means better—far, far, far better than our ways) brings us to the brink of a faith choice—

- Will you stay stuck dreaming about living God's dreams for you?
- Or will you live out the very personal, very specific, very large dreams God has dreamed and is ready to unfold in your life?
- Even if God's dreams seem nightmarishly large, will you step up in faith and put into what God has designed for you into action?

Dreams are the first major image in Joseph's life. A second great image in Joseph's life is that of feast or famine. From Pharaoh's dreams came the prophecy of seven feast years, followed by seven famine years. To shift metaphors from dreams to feasts and famines—

- Will you celebrate the feast God is spreading out before you?
- Or will you only see the distress of the famine you perceive you are enduring?

Here is the truth about living God's dreams—whatever is before you is from God. Whatever is happening in your life—TODAY... RIGHT NOW—is from God. Seemingly good, positively bad, or wholly indifferent—any and all things happening in your life—AT THIS EXACT MOMENT—are from God.

Since your goings-on have been ordained and given to you by God, you are to enjoy and treasure them. You might be tempted to believe you are in the middle of a great famine that is nothing but trouble and terror. However, even from the midst of the negative events taking place in your life, God is providing you a feast, a royal bounty, as only He can.

In the previous chapter, I mentioned my 95-year-old Grandma Ada being hospitalized. As I write the first draft of this chapter, I am flying to Indiana for her funeral. After ten years of separation, my Grandma died and was reunited with my Grandpa (who I talked about in chapter 4) on what would have been their 74th wedding anniversary.

Just as I am figuring out how to write somewhat legibly on the tiny table in seat 11C, the gentleman in the window seat to my left needs to get out to use the lavatory—

- Famine—because I have to stop, unbuckle my seatbelt, gather my papers off the miniature table, stand in the aisle, let him out, and repeat the process in reverse, when he returns?
- Feast—because God's dreams for me (and for this book!) have just been given a brilliant illustration for this chapter?

Either interpretation of events is possible. The event itself is God's gift to me. The choice on how to receive and live out the gift is mine.

Will I grumble, mumble, and, in general, act like the ungrateful Israelites following Moses in the wilderness (see Exodus 15-17 and Numbers 14)?

Or will I take Paul's urging to the conflicted Philippians to heart and—"Rejoice in the Lord always! Again, I say, rejoice!" (Philippians 4:4, NIV).

Another in-flight example, the lady across the aisle checked her messages just before everyone had to power off their electronic devices for take-off. Her iPhone told her the business meeting in Denver she was traveling to had been was pushed back a couple hours for some reason. This news distressed her companion for the entire flight—

- Famine—because their schedule is thrown off?
- Feast—because they have more time to polish their presentation?

Again, the event is God's gift. The choice on how to receive the gift and live it out is theirs.

One more airline example, my seatmate returned from the lavatory and painfully banged his head on the overhead bin. As hard as he hit his head, I have to assume everything inside shifted, so we will have to be very cautious when opening the luggage bin at the end of the flight! His head-banging also caused him to spill a glass of water on the lady sitting in the row in front of us—

- Famine—because now this lady had large water stains on her garish green polyester pantsuit?
- Feast—because. . . well. . . I'm not sure what the feast would be. . .

This is yet another aspect of God's gifts. The gift is always from God. But sometimes the feast from God is not readily apparent. Sometimes what happens to us and to our loved ones is utterly devastating and clearly "bad."

However, God is in charge. God always has a plan. God's plan is greater and grander than anything we can conceive of—remember Joseph!

Even if the only visible effect is that of a famine—God does have a feast in store. Sometimes it might take years to see God's dreams play out into a feast we can genuinely celebrate. Joseph's childhood dreams of brothers bowing before him took decades to be fulfilled.

Still another side to God's gifts is that sometimes the feast is never revealed to us during our lifetime. All we see or think we have received from God is a famine—a terrible, terrible, dark, lonely famine. Even then, God is "The Hero of Faithfulness" and we can live a Philippians 4 life—rejoicing in HIM always.

Sometimes, our life's famines will only be revealed as divine feasts when we are being seated at heaven's ultimate feasting table. Only then will we gain the eyesight to see how God's dreams really were at work in our lives.

What does this mean? As the recipients of God's creative dreams and gifts of grace, we continually have to remind ourselves of the choice we face—

- Feast or famine?
- Live the dream or dream about living?

When the Holy Spirit gives us the grace to choose FEAST and to live out God's dreams, we are able to give God glory in everything—including the glory of extending forgiveness to those who wrong us.

Perhaps Joseph's greatest example of choosing to live out the feast of God's dreams comes after his father, Jacob, dies. Joseph's greatest opportunity to spread the grace of a divine feast comes when his brothers panic.

Showing what happens when we rely on ourselves, with their father Jacob dead, once again, Joseph's brothers connive, finagle, and lie. Filled with haunted memories of what they had done to Joseph all those years before, his brothers tell him—"Dad wanted us to let by-gones be by-gones and live happily ever after."

In Genesis 50, God has presented Joseph another gift. Joseph has a clear choice—vengeance or forgiveness? Does Joseph "stick it to" his brothers, or does he extend grace and forgiveness to them?

Joseph replied to his brothers—

"Don't be afraid. Do I act for God? Don't you see, you planned evil against me but God used those same plans for my good, as you see all around you right now—life for many people. Easy now, you have nothing to fear; I'll take care of you and your children." He reassured them, speaking with them heart-to-heart (Genesis 50:19-21).

Joseph chose the way of grace and forgiveness described in Romans 5—"Sin didn't, and doesn't, have a chance in competition with the aggressive forgiveness we call grace" (Romans 5:20).

Stop and feel the visual interactions of those two words from Romans 5, in your mind's-eye—

- AGGRESSIVE FORGIVENESS

What do you see when you picture those two words joined together?

- AGGRESSIVE FORGIVENESS

Again, God's ways are not our ways. God's dreams for our lives are not usually the same dreams we have for our lives.

Instead of aggressive forgiveness, we are frequently practitioners of aggressive anger and smoldering retribution. Only when circumstances force us, do we make some feeble, lame stabs at forgiveness.

Living out and practicing God's greatest dream for each of us, Joseph shows us the feast of possibilities that exists when we live by a code of "aggressive forgiveness we call grace."

This forgiveness-oriented feast and dream-living helps us bring honor and glory to God in everything we do.

In his song, "Do Everything," Steven Curtis Chapman sings about honoring and glorifying God at all times. Whether the mundane and trivial, or the exciting and outlandish, the choice is ours. Will you "Do Everything" to the glory of God?

> While I may not know you, I bet I know you
> Wonder sometimes, does it matter at all?
> Well let me remind you, it all matters just as long
> As you do everything you do to the glory of the One who made you,
> Cause he made you, To do
> Every little thing that you do
> To bring a smile to His face
> Tell the story of grace
> With every move that you make
> And every little thing you do[1]

Even if your life includes the dark depression and frighteningly fierce famine of witnessing the tragic death of your child, will you—"Do everything you do to the glory of the One who made you, Cause He made you. . ."

Thanks and praise to God that most of the moves we make and the little things we do are far less tragedy-tinged than this.

"Every little thing that you do"—from vacuuming the living room, to enjoying a mug of Safari Sunset tea at a local coffee shop, to volunteering at the public library—is a choice. Will you choose feast. . . or famine?

"Every move that you make"—from the clothes you wear, to the vocation you pursue, to the washing of your dinner dishes—is an opportunity. Will you dream about living. . . or live the dream?

Chapter 11

Moses' Parents: God's Beauty

*W*hen I was in high school, I had a record album (you know. . . the ancient vinyl musical recording devices that came before cassettes. . . which came before CDs. . . which were popular before iTunes. . . and. . . you get the picture. . .). This album was from Christian stand-up comedian Mike Warnke.[1]

I don't remember much from his comic routines. However, one comment from Mike Warnke has stayed with me for well over thirty years. The set up for this punch line was something like this—

Being people who know the joy of redemption and forgiveness from God the Father, in the life, death, and resurrection of Jesus Christ, His only-begotten Son, and having been filled with the power of the Holy Spirit, comedian Mike Warnke couldn't figure out why most Christians walked around looking like they had been sucking on green persimmons.

You know the look he is describing. It is the look perfected by Dana Carvey's "Church Lady" on *Saturday Night Live*. (If you can't recall the "Church Lady". . . rent a video. . . I mean, get a DVD. . . wait. . . just YouTube SNL!)

The look is the very same look that takes over your favorite aunt's face whenever "those topics" come up.

Here is a challenge. . . look around your sanctuary during worship this Sunday and do a quick survey—

- Are there more people whose faces radiate the joy of God's grace?

- Or are there more faces looking like they need to up the dosage of their morning Metamucil?
- Don't forget to check your own face in the mirror before, during, and after taking this survey!

Psalm 33:1-2 declares—"Good people, cheer God! Right-living people sound best when praising. Use guitars to reinforce your Hallelujahs! Play His praise on a grand piano! Invent your own new song to Him; give Him a trumpet fanfare" (Psalm 33:1-2).

I guarantee—if you are cheering God and praising Him, there is absolutely no chance you will look like you've been sucking on green persimmons!

Reading the next verse in Hebrews 11 got me to thinking about the way Christ-followers look. Hebrews 11:23 says—"By an act of faith, Moses' parents hid him away for three months after his birth. They saw the child's beauty, and they braved the king's decree" (Hebrews 11:23).

Of course, all parents believe their baby is the most beautiful baby ever born. I know mine were (Zane and Mallory still are, for that matter!). I'm sure yours were, as well (but I can post on my Facebook page the proof that I'm right!).

- "They saw the child's beauty. . ." (Hebrews 11:23).

What was it about the infant Moses that Hebrews 11 is telling us stood out to his parents?

The original story back in Exodus 2, says—"A man from the family of Levi married a Levite woman. The woman became pregnant and had a son. She saw there was something special about him and hid him. She hid him for three months. . ." (Exodus 2:1-2).

Granted, Moses is the divinely inspired author of Exodus. Given also, is the fact that he is describing his own birth. However, the biases of authorship alone can't explain the word choice. Moses being overly generous to his own legacy as he writes his own story can't explain the feelings of his parents, especially his mother—

- "She saw there was something special about him."

Moses' Parents: God's Beauty

Or as the NIV puts it—

- Moses' mother saw he was "no ordinary child."

Knowing later in life Moses became God's chosen leader for the Exodus makes it easy for us to read the passage and believe the declaration that he was not ordinary. If we put our knowledge of the end of Moses' story before the beginning, it is easy to identify things we believe were special about Moses. Hindsight, as the saying goes, is always 20/20.

What if all we had to go on was Exodus 1&2—then what?

What if we didn't have Exodus 3, or any of the Books of Numbers or Deuteronomy—what then?

What if all we knew about Moses was what Hebrews 11:23 tells us—why does his beauty stand out?

On their own merit, what do these passages tell us about Moses' beauty?

More important, what do these verses show us about God's beauty?

And, how does any of whatever they say apply to us and to our own beauty, especially in the eye of our Divine Beholder?

To begin addressing these questions, let's go to Exodus 1 for a quick look into the context of life in Egypt when Moses was born. Exodus 1 says—

> A new king came to power in Egypt who didn't know Joseph. He spoke to his people in alarm, 'There are way too many of these Israelites for us to handle. We've got to do something: Let's devise a plan to contain them, lest if there's a war they should join our enemies, or just walk off and leave us.' . . . The king of Egypt had a talk with the two Hebrew midwives; one was named Shiphrah and the other Puah. He said, 'When you deliver the Hebrew women, look at the sex of the baby. If it's a boy, kill him; if it's a girl, let her live' (Exodus 1:8-10, 15-16).

The solution to the prolific Hebrew population boom? Slavery and death.

Hebrew babies were to be killed and Hebrew adults were put to hard labor working on the great Egyptian building projects. Over the next forty or so years, the Egyptian recipe for mud bricks devolved, until the Hebrews were making more and more bricks, with less and less supplies.

When Pharaoh saw the Hebrew population boom was continuing, in spite of the hardships he had imposed, he issued a second decree—"Every boy that is born, drown him in the Nile. But let the girls live" (Exodus 1:22).

Put yourself in a Hebrew woman's place—

- Pharaoh decreed death to all baby boys.
- The Hebrew midwives were helping circumvent the law as much as possible (see Exodus 1:15-21).
- Pharaoh then ups the ante to declare even those baby boys born healthy must be drown in the Nile River.
- Every pregnancy had to have been nine exceedingly stressful months.

In this context, "A man from the family of Levi married a Levite woman. . ." (Exodus 2:1).

As is the downward trajectory of human history since Adam and Eve ate the forbidden fruit in the Garden, life in Egypt has become an ugly mess. Life for God's Chosen People under the Egyptian authorities is an ugly mess. They are the slaves being brutalized by Egyptian oppressors. They are having their babies killed.

It cannot be forgotten that life for the Egyptians is also an ugly mess. Real joy for the Egyptian population is not possible when you are brutalizing another people.

At the center of all the ugliness in Egypt is one piece of profound beauty. At the core of everything happening in the Land of Goshen and around the Nile River Delta is the Triune God. At the heart of all life is "The Hero of Faithfulness" who created everything from nothing and declared that everything was—". . . good, so very good!" (Genesis 1:31).

Let's be clear on this—

- The ugly mess of life is totally and completely the fault of and result of human sin.

- Any good or beauty in the world is totally and completely the result of God's presence and grace in the world.

However, grasping for anything to assuage our emotions and guilt, Moses—an innocent, as we would like to believe we also are—is beautiful. We would like to believe beauty is something we can create. At the same time, we subtly (and without conscious thought) equate God with the degeneracy of the world. In other words, God is to blame for any messes in the world.

We think—

- Beauty is our creation and ugly belongs to God.

It is not true. But from the depravity of our sinfulness, we would like it to be so.

In many ways, beautiful, baby Moses being cast into the waters of the Nile is great drama. It is also great foreshadowing. Moses thrown into and then drawn out of those waters is a foreshadowing of Jesus being cast into the womb of Mary and then being drawn into human life as Mary and Joseph's son.

For the better part of a generation, Moses seems to be losing his beauty. When he killed the Egyptian slave master and disappeared into the Midianite wilderness, it appeared "ugly" and sin had won.

Forty years and one burning bush later, Moses was called back from the wilderness to assume the mantle of leadership. With the passage of time, God's story was ready to be advanced from Egypt to the Promised Land.

Beauty is also cast into ugliness for Jesus. Can you imagine what it must have been like for Jesus—the 2nd Person of the Triune God—to leave the right hand of the throne of God the Father in heaven? Whatever you have imagined that event to be like, ratchet up those feelings a few notches when you picture Jesus' face as He learned from His Father that He was going to be born in the muck and mire of a cattle stall.

Thirty-three years later, beauty had only become even more ugly for Jesus. Pharisees and religious leaders were tripping over themselves to plot Jesus' death. Crowds were screaming lustily for His crucifixion. Soldiers were beating Him and spitting on Him.

Of all the degradations and ugliness Jesus endured on His way to the cross, the spit might have been the worst. Power brokers plot to keep power every day. Crowds get riotously carried away all the time. Some punishments can be dispassionately ordered by a superior officer and equally emotionlessly carried out by subordinates.

Not spitting. Spit is disgusting. Spitting is inexcusable. Spitting is foul. Spitting is intentional. Spitting is personal. Spitting is a uniquely gross way of degrading another person.

The contrast of the Passion of Jesus with beautiful baby Moses is described by Isaiah—

> He didn't even look human—a ruined face, disfigured past recognition. . . there was nothing attractive about Him, nothing to cause us to take a second look. He was looked down on and passed over, a man who suffered, who knew pain firsthand. One look at Him and people turned away. We looked down on Him, thought He was scum (Isaiah 52:14, 53:3-4).

Where is "God's Beauty"?

How is this ugly "Suffering Servant" going to save and restore beauty to humankind and all creation?

Precisely because Jesus' story is the greatest story ever, we must continue reading Isaiah's prophecy—

> But the fact is, it was **our pains** He carried—**our disfigurements**, all the things wrong with us. We thought He brought it on Himself, that God was punishing Him for His own failures. But it was **our sins** that did that to Him, that ripped and tore and crushed Him—**our sins**! He took the punishment, and that made us whole. **Through His bruises we get healed** (Isaiah 53:5-6, bold emphasis added).

Still not sure about the divine beauty and purpose to Jesus' ugly death—

> It's what God had in mind all along, to crush [Jesus] with pain. The plan was that [Jesus] give Himself as an offering for sin so

that He'd see life come from it—life, life, and more life. And God's plan will deeply prosper through [Jesus] (Isaiah 53:10).

In Moses' beauty, we see both a foreshadowing of and the reflection of Jesus' beauty. From a reed boat on the waters of the Nile River, through the parted waters of the Red Sea, to the shore of the waters of the Jordan River, Moses reflects God's beauty.

In spite of Jesus' disfigurement and pain, we still are able to see the reflection of God's beautiful salvation plan for His Creation. From His manger in Bethlehem, through His Baptism in the waters of the Jordan River and the temptations in the wilderness, to the beatings, the bloodshed, the cross, the grave—and even through the spit dribbling down His chin—Jesus displays "God's Beauty."

Then comes the most beautiful display of grace and power ever!

Three days after Moses died, he remained dead. Still today, give-or-take 3500 years later, Moses remains buried somewhere outside the Promised Land, in an unmarked and unfound grave.

Jesus, however, died and was buried in Joseph of Arimathea's tomb. Then, after three days enduring death, Jesus rose once and for all from the ignominy of death, back to the beauty of life!

On the first Resurrection Sunday morning, the stone meant to seal Jesus into death and the grave forever was rolled away. The stone was NOT rolled away to let Jesus out of the grave. The stone was rolled away to let us IN on the beauty and grace of resurrection power!

Ephesians 1:19-20 says—"[God's] incomparably great power. . . is like the working of His mighty strength, which He exerted in Christ when He raised Him from the dead and seated Him at His right hand in the heavenly realms" (Ephesians 1:19-20, NIV).

The beauty of God's plan is that by His grace we get to share in His power!

The beauty of Jesus' resurrection is that we are able to live and display this same resurrection beauty and grace and power in all that we do, to do everyone we encounter.

With "God's Beauty" also comes responsibility. To be made beautiful by the life, death, and resurrection of Jesus Christ means—

People are watching us as we stay at our post, alertly, unswervingly. . . in hard times, tough times, bad times. . . with pure heart, clear head, steady hand; in gentleness, holiness, and honest love; when we're telling the truth, and when God's showing His power; when we're doing our best setting things right; when we're praised, and when we're blamed. . . true to our word, though distrusted; ignored by the world, but recognized by God; terrifically alive, though rumored to be dead. . . yet always filled with deep joy. . . (2 Corinthians 6:4-10, selected portions).

Guess what follower of Jesus Christ?
People are watching you.
People who don't know Jesus are looking at you and me.
People who have yet to be eternally affected by "God's Beauty" in Jesus' death and resurrection are studying followers of Jesus Christ.

Since this is so—don't be caught looking like you have been sucking on green persimmons!

I have a pastor friend whose favorite Bible verse is Proverbs 15:13.
Not exactly one you have memorized?
Don't read on until you have looked it up. Read it and highlight it in your Bible (or, at least, bookmark it on your iPhone app!).
Let's etch these words into the contours of our faces—

- "A cheerful heart brings a smile to your face; a sad heart makes it hard to get through the day" (Proverbs 15:13).

If the beauty of Jesus' resurrection and the power of His grace live in your heart, train your face to let it show!

Commit yourself to beautifying the world one smile at a time!

I mentioned my pastor friend a moment ago. Herb and I went to India together on a mission trip a few years ago. We spent two weeks laboring and sweating and working together remodeling a Christian media center.

When the rest of us were wilting in the heat and complaining about the humidity, the smile never left Herb's face. Heat, humidity, pollution, noise, smell, even Delhi Belly (a condition that will make Montezuma seem positively friendly!), you name it—Herb kept smiling.

On our return flight from Chennai, India, to London, England, for nine hours, Herb and I were squeezed together in the middle island of seats. No leg room. No arm room. No breathing room (which didn't matter, because there was no air anyway!). And, still, Herb kept smiling.

Our in-flight meal was served and we tried to gingerly eat our curry without spilling. This delicate ballet worked right up until the moment I spilled an entire bottle of water into Herb's lap.

Miraculously, I did not get a single drop of water on myself!

You guessed it—Herb never stopped smiling.

Sitting with wet pants for several hours—Herb kept on smiling.

Followers of Jesus Christ, people are watching.

We don't have to suppress the joy of our salvation behind persimmon faces.

From the waters of the Nile, to wet pants on the way home from India, the resurrection power of Jesus Christ can make us beautiful witnesses of God's grace in every situation we face.

Raise your right hand. . . SMILE. . . and repeat after me—

- I do solemnly acknowledge. . .
- The power of Jesus' resurrection lives in me!
- I will NOT look like I have been sucking on green persimmons!
- I will train my face to reflect the beauty of God's grace!
- I will smile from now until Jesus comes back. . . and forevermore after that!

Chapter 12

Moses: God's Development

A quick Google search reveals lists of fears and phobias numbering in the 100s.

Some of the more "popular" fears and phobias are—

- Arachnophobia—the fear of spiders
- Acrophobia—the fear of heights
- Claustrophobia—the fear of enclosed spaces
- Brontophobia—the fear of thunder
- Mysophobia—the fear of germs
- Carcinophobia—the fear of cancer
- Necrophobia—the fear of death

The fear that comes closest to being a phobia for me is—

- Ophidiophobia—the fear of snakes

To understand how legitimate the fear of snakes is, it is even recognized by a second name—

- Herpetophobia

I don't like snakes and never have. I joke that the only snake I ever liked was the one made into a pair of Tony Lama snakeskin boots I wore until the sides split out and they couldn't be re-soled again. I still have no idea how my wife got me to go to a rattlesnake museum—on our honeymoon!

How about you? What is it you are afraid of?

Somewhere near the top of every list of fears is one more phobia—

- Glossophobia

Ranging from simple stage-fright, to a stomach feeling full of nervous butterflies, to hug-the-toilet nausea, to absolute panic and immobilizing terror, glossophobia affects countless people and cripples many of them. Quite simply, glossophobia is the fear of public speaking.

Moving from Moses' Parents in the last chapter, to a look at the life of Moses, himself, in this chapter, fears and phobias lurk all throughout the Book of Exodus.

As we focus on Moses, Hebrews 11:24-28 narrow our attention to the central pieces in his story. *The Message* renders these verses like this—

> By faith, Moses, when grown, refused the privileges of the Egyptian royal house. He chose a hard life with God's people rather than an opportunistic soft life of sin with the oppressors. He valued suffering in the Messiah's camp far greater than Egyptian wealth because he was looking ahead, anticipating the payoff. By an act of faith, he turned his heel on Egypt, indifferent to the king's blind rage. He had his eye on the One no eye can see, and kept right on going. By an act of faith, he kept the Passover Feast and sprinkled Passover blood on each house so that the destroyer of the firstborn wouldn't touch them (Hebrews 11:24-28).

A quick review of Moses' life finds a drama playing itself out in three chronologically equal acts—

- Age 1-40: Raised in Pharaoh's courts and trained in Egyptian culture, history, and ways.

- Age 41-80: Living in the Midianite wilderness learning the topography and terrain of the desert, while running his father-in-law's flocks.
- Age 81-120: Leading the Children of Israel out of Egypt, through the Red Sea, around the wilderness, to the brink of entering the Promised Land.

These three phases in Moses' life reveal yet another dimension of the character of our "Hero of Faithfulness." In each stage of Moses' life, God reveals that He is intricately interested in how Moses develops and grows as a human being. Beyond everything else, God is concerned with the development and growth of Moses' character, as well as, your character and mine.

Saint Paul speaks about the development of godly character and virtues in Colossians 3—

> Since, then, you have been raised with Christ, set your hearts on things above, where Christ is seated at the right hand of God. Set your minds on things above, not on earthly things. For you died, and your life is now hidden with Christ in God... Therefore, as God's chosen people, holy and dearly loved, clothe yourselves with compassion, kindness, humility, gentleness and patience. Bear with each other and forgive whatever grievances you may have against one another. Forgive as the Lord forgave you. And over all these virtues put on love, which binds them all together in perfect unity (Colossians 3:1-3, 12-14, NIV).

Unfortunately, as a result of our sinful nature, we live as if we are clothed in anything but these godly and Christ-like virtues. Left to our own devices, we much more resemble these verses of Colossians 3—

> Whatever belongs to your earthly nature: sexual immorality, impurity, lust, evil desires and greed, which is idolatry. Because of these, the wrath of God is coming. You used to walk in these ways, in the life you once lived. But now you must rid yourselves of all such things as these: anger, rage, malice,

slander, and filthy language from your lips. Do not lie to each other... (Colossians 3:5-9, NIV).

The character development God aims to work in every one of us will see us move from a life wallowing in filth and frustration, to living a life with a heart set on God-pleasing motives. This is also the character development we find God executing throughout the three stages of Moses' life.

Come on a journey back to Egypt, as we walk through Moses' century of living.

Once he was drawn out of the Nile River's water by Pharaoh's daughter, Moses had every luxury Egyptian royalty could throw at him. For the first forty years of his life, Moses lived in the opulence and advantage of the Egyptian royal house.

Moses enjoyed the most, best, and finest foods. He was taught by the smartest and brightest scholars. If an insight or advantage was available, Moses was educated in it. He had knowledge of every technology and discovery from around the globe.

However, as Moses' childhood passed into his early adult years, a sense of unrest began to grow in him. Moses knew he wasn't Egyptian. Moses knew Hebrew blood flowed through his veins. From his elevated and protected palace view, Moses saw his people being brutally oppressed. As an extra kicker, Moses also knew he should have died in the purge of Hebrew babies ordered by his step-father.

Eventually, the competing Egyptian and Hebrew cultures collided. Finally, the tension inside Moses exploded when he killed an Egyptian taskmaster who was beating a Hebrew slave.

In an intriguing choice of phrases, Hebrews 11 says—"By faith, Moses, when grown, refused the privileges of the Egyptian royal house. He chose a hard life with God's people rather than an opportunistic soft life of sin with the oppressors" (Hebrews 11:24).

Murder followed by flight hardly seems like a refusal of "the privileges of the Egyptian royal house." But maybe it was.

Consider—with the full authority of the Egyptian Pharaoh behind him, any punishment Moses may have received from his rash action would have likely been little more than a proverbial "slap on the wrist." Moses would have enjoyed diplomatic immunity as if he were Pharaoh's own flesh and blood.

Instead of claiming the privileges of Egyptian royalty, Moses chose to flee into the Midianite wilderness. When faced with a crisis of the first degree, Moses did refuse to claim all the rights and privileges of his Egyptian adoption. Instead, this first phase of his character development saw Moses driven away from both the Egyptian and Hebrew cultures. Moses fled from Egypt and Israel for forty years living in yet another culture—the nomadic, sheepherding ways of the desert.

While Tim McGraw sings about making significant changes in his "Next 30 Years," Moses really did make changes in his second forty years. According to Hebrews 11, Moses second forty years were spent in "a hard life."

From the age of forty to eighty, Moses learned the wandering, hard-scrabble life of the wilderness. He learned the locations of all the desert's watering holes. He learned how to negotiate the dangers of the trade routes. He learned how to deal with the differences in the seasons, as well as searing heat by day and bone-chilling cold at night.

In his role as a sheepherder for a Midianite priest, Moses labored and sweat and learned everything there was to know about the "hard life." So thoroughly did Moses become engrossed in the nomadic life of the desert, he even married the desert priest's daughter.

The first forty years of Moses' life were all about higher learning, intellectual debate, and accumulating skills and privileges. For his first four decades, Moses never missed a manicure as he lived the "soft life."

The second forty years of Moses' life were all about blood, sweat, and tears. Moses' second set of four decades saw him develop callouses and blisters on his hands and feet. Moses learned what it meant to live with a sore back following a hard day's work. More than once, the sweat of Moses' brow stung his eyes as he stared into shimmering heat waves. For forty years, Moses chose "a hard life."

These two very different phases of Moses' life set him up for a final act that only God could have envisioned. As Hebrews 11 puts it, the Moses alive from age 80-120 would have been more astounded than anyone to see how God was using him—"By an act of faith... [Moses] kept the Passover Feast and sprinkled Passover blood on each house so that the destroyer of the firstborn wouldn't touch them" (Hebrews 11:28).

"God's Development" of Moses' character is reflected in the action words *The Message* uses in Hebrews 11 to describe him.

Moses—

- **Refused** privilege. . .
- **Chose** a hard life with God's people. . .
- **Valued** suffering. . .
- **Turned** his heel on Egypt. . .
- **Kept** the Passover. . .
- **Sprinkled** Passover blood. . .

Yet, fears and phobias almost kept Moses from being fertile soil for "God's Development."

When God first appeared to Moses in "The Burning Bush," Moses tried every argument possible to escape being used as God's instrument. For all his arguments against going back to Egypt, Moses' last gasp excuse was—"Master, please, I don't talk well. I've never been good with words, neither before nor after You spoke to me. I stutter and stammer" (Exodus 4:10).

Rearing its ugly head is that fear on every list—

- Glossophobia—the fear of public speaking

Moses tries to tell God he don't talk so good. (Interesting, however, that Moses' own construction of the event as he wrote it under the Holy Spirit's inspiration some years later, is both eloquent and grammatically correct!).

In effect, God responds to Moses' glossophobia, saying—"Puh-lease! Is that the best you can come up with? I AM God. . . I AM going to do the talking! If, however, you are going to be this lame, I AM going to send your brother Aaron with you."

With that divine revelation, Moses got up from the burning bush, put his sandals back on, and returned to Egypt. Following forty years in the wilderness, Moses began the struggle to convince his Hebrew culture God had sent him to their rescue. After being absent from

Egypt for four decades, Moses also had to convince his Egyptian culture that the Hebrew God had sent him to lead their best slaves out of oppression and bondage.

From years in Egyptian royalty, to decades in the wilderness, Moses "has his eye on the One no eye can see." From his "soft life of sin with the oppressors," to "a hard life with God's people," Moses shows us how God never stops working to develop His character in His children.

The example of "God's Development" of Moses begs the question—

- What characteristic does God need to develop in you?

"God's Development" of character and virtue in us has two sides. On one side are the "soft life of sin" characteristics needing to be eliminated from us. On the other side are the "hard life" characteristics needing to be developed in us.

At first glance it may appear I have my "hards" and "softs" confused. But look closer at the characteristics listed in Colossians 3. The "soft" (and sinful) virtues needing to be put to death are—

> ...sexual immorality, impurity, lust, evil desires and greed, which is idolatry. Because of these, the wrath of God is coming. You used to walk in these ways, in the life you once lived. But now you must rid yourselves of all such things as these: anger, rage, malice, slander, and filthy language from your lips. Do not lie to each other... (Colossians 3:12-14, NIV).

The "hard" (and godly!) characteristics needing to become part of our spiritual wardrobe and make-up are—

> ...compassion, kindness, humility, gentleness and patience. Bear with each other and forgive whatever grievances you may have against one another. Forgive as the Lord forgave you. And over all these virtues put on love, which binds them all together in perfect unity... (Colossians 3:5-9a, 12-14, NIV).

It might appear calling "soft" traits like impurity, lust, greed, and all the rest, is inaccurate. But the reality is all evil characteristics embody easy, soft choices. It takes no spine or heart to give in and fall down the slimy slope into the depravity Colossians 3 describes.

Likewise, calling compassion, humility, patience, and love "hard" might fly in the face of logic. Yet to be clothed in the virtues Colossians describes requires the hard, persevering work of faith. These Godly virtues all need the ongoing development lived out of the crucible of the Holy Spirit's lead.

Given this contrast of "hard" and "soft" virtues, let me ask again—

- Knowing yourself as only you know you. . . what does God need to develop into or out of you?

It is interesting to note that Paul continues his argument in Colossians 3:15 with this encouragement—"Let the peace of Christ rule in your hearts, since as members of one body you were called to peace" (Colossians 3:15, NIV).

This verse raises another challenging question—

- How can we have peace—of any kind. . . let alone, "the peace of Christ"—if we are constantly wrestling with the "soft" and "hard" choices of our character's development?

The answer actually is—easily. At least, it is easy to have peace once we understand the true nature of peace.

Go back to Moses. Once he returned to Egypt, his life became extremely challenging. For his last forty years, he did not have an easy go of things. First, he faced repeated confrontations with Pharaoh (either his step-father, or at least, some level of a step-relative of his). He also endured constant pressure from the Hebrews (his blood-kin). Don't forget the stress of living through (and being seen by many as the CAUSE of) all the plagues, death, and destruction. And all of this trouble and hardship before even getting out of Egypt and into the wilderness with all the Israelites!

Our greatest misconception about peace is believing true peace resides only in the absence of trouble or conflict. We mistakenly equate peace with ease. But it is not.

Much like our confusion of "soft" and "hard" virtues, we are confused about the nature of true peace. True peace that God desires to have ruling our hearts (and, therefore, our lives) is NOT the absence of trouble or conflict. True peace derives from the hope and security arising solely from the knowledge that our life is clothed with the righteousness of Christ.

Even amid all the swirl and chaos of the plagues and political realities, Moses was able to maintain true peace because he was secure in his relationship with "I AM," "The Hero of Faithfulness" who had chosen him and revealed His Name at the Burning Bush.

Likewise, when conflict and turmoil, or pain and problems, rage all around, you can know and live true peace. When you live as a member of the body of Christ, true peace and godly character will grow in you. When you are clothed in the righteous robes of Christ's death and resurrection, you will enjoy true peace and "God's Development" of your character.

Eventually, after the darkness and death of the tenth plague, Moses led the people out of Egypt. Instead of a swift hike to safety, they walked right to the brink of another disaster at the Red Sea. With trouble and conflict pressing him on all sides, Moses maintained his composure and lived filled with true peace.

Visualize the scene. . .

Pharaoh and the Egyptian army were pressing from the west. The Red Sea was in front of him to the west. The Hebrews were freaking out all around him. But Moses (with no hint of his glossophobia) eloquently took center stage and declared—"Don't be afraid. Stand firm and watch God do His work of salvation for you today. Take a good look at the Egyptians today for you're never going to see them again. God will fight the battle for you." (Exodus 14:13-14).

In effect, Moses spoke to the Israelites, but declared to God—"God, I don't care where we go. . . or how we get there. . . as long as YOU go with us!"

That kind of peace is the ultimate character development God is seeking to build in each of us!

So—

- What is God seeking to develop in you?

And—

- Will you trust that what He is developing in you is what is best for you?
- Will you trust that whatever God has in store for you will bring you the "true peace of Christ"?

Chapter 13

Israel & The Red Sea: God's Glory

*E*ither an unnamed medieval monk, 20th century mystic Thomas Merton, or Jobonanno and the Godsons, first said—

- "God draws straight with crooked lines."[1]

Regardless of the original speaker, many variations on this theme have been uttered through the centuries.

The meaning of this saying is bound up in the miraculous ability of God to glorify Himself by using the clutter and craziness of our lives for His divine purposes.

We wander through life like a child randomly picking daisies, while at the same time trying to kick a can down a path, all as we simultaneously hold onto a parent's hand. Through the vagaries of our wanderings, God is accomplishing in and through us the straightforward, divine desires He doodled onto heaven's whiteboard before time even began ticking.

With Moses having led the Israelites out of Egypt, the author of Hebrews 11 takes a "crooked line" for the next two verses. For 28 verses, Hebrews 11 has marked a straightforward path talking about God's faithfulness to one individual after another.

Hebrews 11:29-30, however, do not detail God's faithfulness to any single person. Instead, these two verses illuminate two events involving the entire nation of Israel—the Red Sea crossing and the tumbling down of Jericho's walls.

In this chapter, we will see how the Red Sea crossing provides "The Hero of Faithfulness" the perfect forum to put "God's Glory," as well as, His miraculous abilities and power on display.

In the next chapter, God will invite the Israelites to join Him in miraculously bringing the walls of Jericho down and shining His Glory even more brightly.

The last chapter ended with Moses declaring—"Don't be afraid. Stand firm and watch God do His work of salvation for you today. Take a good look at the Egyptians today for you're never going to see them again. God will fight the battle for you. . ." (Exodus 14:13-14).

Reading all of Exodus 14 shows that the context for Moses' words was what the ungrateful Israelites perceived to be a "crooked line." Instead of leaving Egypt behind and quickly traveling east and north up the Mediterranean coast to freedom in the Promised Land, God led the Children of Israel east and south into the wilderness. The people—none of whom had ever seen the world outside Egypt—belligerently believed they knew geography and travel details better than God!

Regardless of where they were, or how they got there, God had a plan. Instead of trust in the God who had miraculously delivered them from the Angel of Death's midnight rampage through Egypt, the people panicked.

> The Israelites looked up and saw them—Egyptians! Coming at them! They were totally afraid. They cried out in terror to God. They told Moses, 'Weren't the cemeteries large enough in Egypt so that you had to take us out here in the wilderness to die? What have you done to us, taking us out of Egypt? Back in Egypt didn't we tell you this would happen? Didn't we tell you, "Leave us alone here in Egypt—we're better off as slaves in Egypt than as corpses in the wilderness"' (Exodus 14:10-14).

As they wandered the wilderness in a "crooked line," the Children of Israel couldn't see that God had a "straight line," straightforward reason for leading them out into the wilderness. God was making—"sure the Egyptians keep up their stubborn chase" (Exodus 14:17).

To go north through Philistia probably would have stopped the Egyptians from following them. Traveling north also would have exposed the Hebrews to a war with a new enemy. Even more than a battle against an unknown foe that they would have been ill-equipped to fight, God wanted to "use Pharaoh and his entire army, his chariots and horsemen, to put My Glory on display so that the Egyptians will realize that I am God" (Exodus 14:17-18).

Putting "God's Glory" on display so that someone—anyone and everyone!—realizes He alone is God should suffice as a reason for anything and everything that happens in our lives. Regardless of what happens to us, we can trust and be certain that God is always at work putting His Glory on display to draw someone closer to Himself.

Back in Egypt, before, during, and after every plague, Moses gained an audience with Pharaoh. Over and over again, speaking on God's behalf, Moses never said to Pharaoh—"Let my people go PERIOD..."

Moses always declared to Pharaoh—"Let my people go COMMA..."

Getting out of Egypt was always only one step along the way toward a greater goal. The goal Moses always communicated to Pharaoh was—"Let my people go COMMA that they may worship God."

Certainly, the Hebrews thought escape from Egyptian tyranny was the greatest need they had. However, God—as always!—had bigger and greater goals in mind.

Just a few days out of Egypt and the Israelites have thrown "God's Glory" into the wind. Only a brief while into the wilderness and worship is far from their heart, mind, or soul. Only hopelessness and despair are visible to them. Only fear and doom are on their minds. So quickly have things gone south, the Israelites are longing for the oppressive, slave life they had only so recently left behind in Egypt.

Thankfully, God kept faithful to Himself and to His ideals.

Fortunately, God persisted in pursuing His plan.

With Egyptian chariots quickly closing in from the west and with the Red Sea blocking them to the east, God gloriously led Israel to safety. You know the miracle—

- Moses stretched out his hand...
- God blew a mighty wind that parted the waters...

- The Israelites—all 600,000+ of them and their animals and all they had plundered from Egypt—walked through the Red Sea on dry ground.
- Miracle upon miracle—not a single drop of water splashed on them. . . nor was there a speck of mud to be found on any of their sandals!
- Then—Moses stretched his hand back over the Red Sea. . .
- And—"As the day broke and the Egyptians were running, the sea returned to its place as before. God dumped the Egyptians in the middle of the sea. The waters returned, drowning the chariots and riders of Pharaoh's army that had chased after Israel into the sea. Not one of them survived" (Exodus 14:28).

As they stood on the far side of the Red Sea, stunned by what had just happened, the Israelites—"looked at the Egyptian dead, washed up on the shore of the sea, and realized the tremendous power that God brought against the Egyptians. The people were in reverent awe before God and trusted in God and His servant Moses" (Exodus 14:30-31).

The line from Egypt to (and through) the Red Sea may have seemed crooked, but God had drawn straight to His goals—

- His Chosen Nation was freed from bondage in Egypt!
- "God's Glory" was put on display for the whole world to see in the greatest miracle to that point!
- And, His People worshiped in the wilderness as originally intended!

As they began to realize the full weight of what had just happened, Moses and the Israelites sang and danced and worshiped—

I will sing to the Lord, for He is highly exalted. The horse and its rider He has hurled into the sea. The Lord is my strength and my song; He has become my salvation. He is my God, and I will praise Him, my father's God, and I will exalt Him. The Lord is a warrior; the Lord is His name. Pharaoh's chariots and his army He has hurled into the sea. The best of Pharaoh's officers are drowned in the Red Sea. The deep waters have covered them; they sank to the depths like a stone. Your right hand, O Lord, was majestic in power. Your right hand, O Lord, shattered the enemy (Exodus 15:1-6, NIV).

Are you ready to apply the Red Sea miracle to your life? As you think about "God's Glory," especially as revealed in the Red Sea—

- What is your view of God?

This question is not thrown at you out of left field (nor is it just another crooked twist in the seemingly random path this chapter is taking). In these early 21st century years, there are many misunderstandings about God and His nature.

Quite a few of the misconceptions people have of God center on trying to turn Him into some kind of "Holy Vending Machine."

Like a sentinel in a wide hallway, God stands silent. From a distant corner, He waits passively in the shadows for our approach. When we feel an urge, He offers us several choices. After comparing and considering, we make a selection. We insert a few coins. We press a button or two. And, voila! God gives us what we want. God's usefulness then ends as we walk away. We leave Him a cold, mute machine until the next time we need Him.

If, by chance (or by bad theology!), we prefer a God who is a bit more animated, there is the "Divine MacGyver" approach to God.

If you remember the television adventure series from the late 1980s and early 1990s, MacGyver was a secret agent for a shadowy and specialized United States government agency. MacGyver was also a pacifist who refused to touch a gun. As he raced through hailstorms of bullets in each episode, MacGyver needed a creative, non-violent way to bring resolution to the situation. Somehow, MacGyver was always able to fashion an escape and answer to every problem that arose using some combination of duct tape, a Swiss Army knife, a paper clip, and any random fourth object.

For some people, their view of God is that of a "Divine MacGyver." In any situation, God can overcome whatever obstacle we put in His way with just a few simple household ingredients. And with all the colored rolls of duct tape now available at your local Wal-Mart, God can even be stylish and fashionable as He gets us out of our sticky situations!

Let me pose the question again—

- What is your view of God?

Selfishly creating a God who can save the day—or at least meet your wants and impulses—with paper clips and duct tape won't suffice.

Seeking a God who bows low and serves your whims and wishes like a "Divine Butler" or a "Cosmic Therapist" will leave you lost.

Only a God who continually puts His Glory on display in truly immense, universe-changing miracles—like the Red Sea crossing. . . or like Jericho's tumbling walls—is capable of drawing straight with the crooked lines of your life.

Only a God who puts His Glory on display in miracles—like the Red Sea or the Battle of Jericho—is capable of being present and powerful in the "mundane" miracles your daily life requires.

Only the God of the Exodus is worthy of your worship and praise because, as Ephesians 3 says, only—HE IS ABLE!

As Paul prays for the followers of Christ in Ephesus, he makes this declaration about God's Glory and miraculous abilities—

> Now to Him who is able to do immeasurably more than all we ask or imagine, according to His power that is at work within us, to Him be glory in the church and in Christ Jesus throughout all generations, for ever and ever! Amen (Ephesians 3:20-21, NIV).

Just stop and think about the depth and breadth and weight of those first six words—

- "Now to Him who is able. . ."

Out in the wilderness with Egyptians chasing them into a corner, the Israelites were being led by the God "who is able."

Likewise, in the crooked corners of your life where you think only a miracle will get you out, you can take comfort! You have in your corner the God "who is able."

In the barren wilderness of your life, this is not—

- The God who sometimes can. . .
- The God who occasionally might. . .
- The God who recently began. . .
- The God who really tries. . .

Just as the Israelites over 3000 years ago, we are under the power and provision of the "God who is able. . ."

Here is what I want you to do—

I want you to take this book with you to your favorite "Contemplation Corner."

I want you to get comfortable for a few minutes.

I want you to allow each of these next statements to slowly roll through your mind, touching the depths of your emotions. . .

I want you to allow the scope and breadth of each of these miracles to shape your view of God. . .

Ready?

Set?

Comfortable?

- God is able. . . to make the aurora borealis dance. . .
- God is able. . . to cause Pleiades and Orion to twinkle. . .
- God is able. . . to form human brains out of over 100 billion individual nerve cells. . .
- God is able. . . to release in women a hormone that causes the pain of childbirth to wash away in a flood of nurturing love. . .
- God is able. . . to place an average of 100,000 hairs on the heads of each of His children. . .
- God is able. . . to see you through the wilderness of your problems. . .

The list of what God is able to do could go on and on. . .

Let these next three statements really knock you out with God's abilities.

Are you still comfortable and ready to feel the weighty fullness of "God's Glory"?

First—

- God is able... to part the waters of the Red Sea so the Hebrew nation can escape the Egyptians AND so His people can worship Him!

Second—

- God is able... to bring down the walls of Jericho so His Children can conquer their foes AND so they can worship Him!

Third—

- God is able... to raise His only-begotten Son, Jesus Christ, to life, from death, so all humankind can know their sins have been atoned for and life eternal can be theirs AND so we can worship Him!

The "Holy Hairdresser God" so many seek advice from can perform many miracles with hair dye and other tricks of the cosmetology trade. However, no perm or pigment is a match for what God is able to do.

Likewise, the "Divine Bartender God" so many people pull up a barstool before finds his tap has gone dry in the face of truly divine miracles.

Here is what "God's Glory" means for you and me. Here is what Hebrews 11:23 is trying to tell us—

- God is able to draw straight with the crooked lines of your life!
- God is able to perform miracles in the darkest corners of your life!

The "Hero of Faithfulness" is able to accomplish His purposes even from the confusion of your life!

Think you have done something too far off course for God to redirect—He is able!

Think you have done something too heinous for Him to redeem—He is able!

Think you are not worthy of His attention—He is able!

Just like the Children of Israel who were complaining about His incompetence, God wants to use you in spite of your wanderings. God wants to put His Glory on display in you. God wants to receive your worship and praise. God wants to unleash His miraculous power into your life.

You are the vehicle God wants to drive His miracles through!

You are the person God wants to shine His Glory through!

You are the source God wants to hear singing and dancing and worshiping—

I'm singing my heart out to God—what a victory! He pitched horse and rider into the sea. God is my strength, God is my song, and, yes! God is my salvation. *This* is the kind of God I have and I'm telling the world! *This* is the God of my father—I'm spreading the news far and wide! (Exodus 15:1-2, italics in original).

Chapter 14

Israel & Jericho: God's Posture

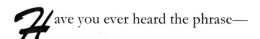

*H*ave you ever heard the phrase—

- Carefree Timelessness[1]

I came across this phrase in an email newsletter some time ago. The more I have thought about the relationship between these two words, the more I believe "carefree timelessness" is an extremely rare commodity today. I also believe "carefree timeless" is critical for our spiritual well-being.

"Carefree timelessness" refers to spending periods of time in relaxed settings with friends and family members.

"Carefree timelessness" is quantities of time spent without structure, or the pressure of a schedule.

"Carefree timelessness," in decades gone by, is probably what was called "leisure time."

"Carefree timelessness" is an evening spent lounging on the front porch listening to a baseball game on the radio.

"Carefree timelessness" is an afternoon spent leaning on the white picket fence between backyards catching up with the neighbors.

"Carefree timelessness" is what farmers practice when they pull their pick-ups next to each other in the middle of a country road, roll down the windows, and talk about crops until the cows come home.

The essence of "carefree timelessness" requires—

- Chunks of time...
- With NO agenda...
- And NO time pressures...

In our warp-drive, hyper-competitive world, "carefree timelessness" might be the rarest of all jewels today!

We like to believe we are all under intense time pressure. It is only 8:11am, as I write this in a booth at a local restaurant. I have already heard three people sigh and sputter some variation of—"Gotta get going, or I'll be running behind all day..."

Not only do we believe we are under crushing time pressure, most of us have too many things on our agendas. If we would stop competing for "Busiest Social Calendar," many of us might just have to admit, we really don't need Google calendars to schedule our day down to 15-minute (or less!) blocks of time.

Which leads to the most difficult piece of the "carefree timelessness" puzzle to guard—chunks of time.

- Chunks of time—not fragments hurried between phone calls, texts, and emails.
- Blocks of time—not pieces squeezed between the race from one stoplight to the next.

When applied spiritually, the point of "carefree timelessness" is that for the well-being of our relationship with Almighty God, we need to regularly set aside our agendas and time constraints. Instead of hurrying through our busy-ness, we need to lose ourselves in chunks of time with God—

- Take a walk—a leisurely stroll, not an exercise-induced power-walk designed to get your heart-rate to a desired level... but an aimless, random, lengthy walk around the neighborhood...
- Write (by hand!) a letter—with pen and ink! Not another meaningless 140 character tweet or text...

- Read your Bible—whole chapters. . . not a proof-text based, 250-word devotion gulped down between swallows of stale coffee. . .

"Carefree timelessness"—the words sound warm and inviting as they roll off your tongue.

"Carefree timelessness" is integral to the second of Hebrews 11's "crooked line" verses.

In the last chapter, Hebrews 11:29 talked of "God's Glory" revealed in the miraculous event of the Red Sea crossing. Now, in this chapter, Hebrews 11:30 will speak about "God's Posture" in relation to the Israelites and the walls of Jericho.

Hebrews 11:29-30 turn our attention to "The Hero of Faithfulness" shaping and molding His followers through the use of His divinely miraculous powers. "God's Glory" is revealed through His miraculous power at the Red Sea. "The Hero of Faithfulness" then invites the Israelites to join in the implementation of the next miracle. The Israelites are not just going to be the recipients of a miracle. They are expressly invited to believe, follow, and participate in God's miraculous plans.

Turn for a refresher on the events around Jericho to Joshua 6. In the first two verses, Scripture tells us—"Jericho was shut up tight as a drum because of the People of Israel: no one going in, no one coming out. God spoke to Joshua, 'Look sharp now. I've already given Jericho to you, along with its king and its crack troops'" (Joshua 6:1-2).

Turn off the "Veggie Tales" images of ice cream bombs splatting on the Israelites' heads. Put away your old flannel-board Sunday School images. Instead, translate your mind from the 21st century AD, back to about 1500 BC.

As Israel camped near Jericho, the setting was terrifying. Forty years wandering in the wilderness had passed since they crossed the Red Sea. Moses and an entire generation had died. Joshua was now in charge. The people had entered the Promised Land (with a "mini Red Sea-like" parting of the Jordan River's waters). Now, they were camped outside Jericho and things looked bleak.

THE Hero of Faithfulness

The reason for the forty year wilderness sabbatical was God's punishment following the debacle of Israel's covert mission spying on Canaan.

Remember? Twelve spies went into the land. Ten came back dazzled by the land's potential, but certain they (and their God!) were too weak to possess the land. Only Joshua and Caleb stood tall and declared God's victory over the people in the land would be their victory. As a result of the people siding with the majority of the spies, God declared death to a generation before He would lead anyone into the Promised Land.

So here they finally are. Forty years later. A new generation of Israelites under Joshua's leadership. Joshua was freshly strengthened by an encounter with the commander of the Lord's Army (see Joshua 5). But their first fight was going to be against Jericho.

Jericho was a walled city, with no ordinary walls. Jericho's walls were fifty feet tall and at least ten feet thick. Jericho's walls not only had apartments for the citizens to live in built into them, these walls had the chariots of Jericho's army patrolling along the top of them.

Still God spoke to Joshua and said, "I've already given Jericho to you. . ." (Joshua 6:2).

The descendants of at least ten Israelite spies and more than a few others whose parents and grandparents had died in the wilderness had to have wondered—"Forty years in the desert. . . and now this?"

The city was impenetrable! Its walls appeared impregnable!
Fear not!
God had a plan—

- Follow seven silent priests carrying seven ram's horns around the city. . .
- Have all the soldiers in the army silently follow the priests around the city once a day for six days. . .
- On day seven, follow the priests silently around the city six more times. . .
- Then make a seventh trip around the city blowing trumpets and shouting. . .
- "The city wall will collapse at once. All the people are to enter, every man straight on in" (Joshua 6:5).

Can you hear the offspring of the ten spies leading a chorus of head-shaking—"Yeah, right! Who is this Joshua guy, anyway? I thought Moses had some nutty ideas! Nothing like several silent strolls to scare Jericho's inhabitants into surrendering!"

If you were standing there that day listening to Joshua, it would have been tempting to say—"What is God thinking? Thirteen quiet strolls around the city, followed by a few trumpet blasts and shouts. What will that accomplish? At least, Moses could be counted on to smash a stick on the rocks, or bust up the tablets God gave him!"

Perhaps a more traditional attack involving building some siege works and ramparts might have a greater chance at success?

Maybe a few months spent working on becoming proficient with catapults and flaming arrows?

After God spoke to Joshua, Joshua immediately—and faithfully—led the people into the implementation of God's plan.

"And it happened" (Joshua 6:8).

The Israelites faithfully followed Joshua and the seven priests around the city. On the seventh trip of the seventh day, trumpets blew and people shouted. "The Hero of Faithfulness" faithfully brought the walls of Jericho tumbling down.

Once again, God performed a spectacular miracle that put His Glory on display. Not only that, this time the entire nation got to participate in the execution of God's miracle.

As "God's Glory" stood tall, the walls of Jericho fell flat.

When God's people stood tall in their faith, "God's Glory" shone bright.

This is what the divine characteristic of "God's Posture" is all about. Hebrews 11 includes Jericho alongside the Red Sea because "God's Posture" is to stand tall and shine His Glory through His miracles for His people—even if the ways and means to achieving the miracles seem slightly crooked!

When analyzing the miracle at Jericho, we could get caught up in countless strategic questions—

- Why not retreat from Jericho and attack a different Canaanite city?
- Why seven priests and why seven days?

- Why thirteen total trips around Jericho?
- Why trumpets and not harps?
- Why silence until the very end?

God's means to accomplishing this miracle make absolutely no logical or rational sense. Which is almost certainly the point!

No one—neither Joshua, nor Caleb, nor any of the seven priests, not one single Israelite—no one of Israelite descent could claim Jericho's immense and impressive walls came tumbling down because of their military effort or strategic brilliance.

"God's Posture"—alone—stood tall and brought Jericho low.

For our hurried and harried lives, the seven time-consuming days walking around Jericho are important. In our world of busy-ness and over-scheduling, thirteen slow strolls around Jericho are significant—

- We feel overwhelmed.
- We always seem to be out of time.
- We want God to get a move on and take care of everything—ASAP (if not sooner)!

But God doesn't operate that way.

Hebrews 11's "Hero of Faithfulness" is a God of "carefree timelessness." "God's Posture" at Jericho is that of a relaxed and creative God. Our God has an agenda. He wants everyone to know Him and to shine with His Glory. But He will not be pressured by our hurried-ness into rushing His plans.

To become participants in God's miracles today, we need to assume better posture. Instead of slouching toward Gomorrah and impatiently demanding God act NOW, we need to adopt the posture described in 1 Timothy 6:11.

As his first letter to his protégé comes to a close, Paul gives Timothy some advice. *The Message* renders Paul's advice to Timothy this way—"Pursue a righteous life—a life of wonder, faith, love, steadiness, courtesy" (1 Timothy 6:11).

With minor variations, the majority of other translations render the verse as the New King James does—"Pursue righteousness, godliness, faith, love, patience, gentleness" (1 Timothy 6:11, NKJV).

What *The Message* calls "a righteous life" that consists in the pursuit of "wonder, faith, love, steadiness, courtesy," is, in most other translations, a list of values and qualities that begins with the pursuit of "righteousness, godliness, faith. . ."

Only *The Message* uses the word "wonder" to describe the pursuit of godliness. Once again, either Eugene Peterson is taking liberties with the text. Or he is helping us in a very insightful way to see across the centuries into God's original designs for righteousness.

- "Pursue a life of wonder. . ."

The use of the word "wonder" slows us down. If only to cause us to say, "I wonder what He means?"

Godliness cannot be attained in an afternoon.

The wonder of godliness can only be pursued by a slow, steady lifetime of faith and love. The wonder of godliness takes enough time and focus that we become—by the leading of the Holy Spirit—able to see God's great and mighty miracles for what they are. God's great and glorious miracles are reminders of His intimate presence in the "small" miracles that surround us every minute of every day.

The parting of the Red Sea and the tumbling down of Jericho's walls are divine reminders that "The Hero of Faithfulness" is concerned with every breath we take and with every decision we make. God desperately desires that we slow down and see how He is the God of the details—our details!

When thought of like this, Paul's advice to Timothy almost sounds like encouragement to allow God to "draw straight with the crooked lines" of our lives. It almost sounds as if we are being called to pursue a life of "carefree timelessness." It sounds like advice to slow down, be patient, and to assume a posture of participation in God's plans.

Here is another truism concerning the miracle at Jericho—

- Israel's seven days walking around Jericho could absolutely not be hurried.

If Joshua had tried to cram thirteen trips around the city into just two or three days, there would have been no miracle.

If Joshua had become impatient and signaled the priests to blow the trumpets and shout after just six trips on the seventh day, there would have been no miracle.

Fully and completely growing up in "God's Posture" and patient plan was imperative to the completion of the miracle.

God is not interested in us short-circuiting things. Joshua and Israel had a specific process to follow. So also God wants us to walk through the entire process of His miraculous presence and provision in our lives.

Pursuing a life of wonder can't be squeezed into a 15-minute window late in the afternoon on the third Thursday of every other month. The wonder of "carefree timelessness" takes chunks of time free from the confines of an agenda set on "advancing the ball" and forcing progress toward some ill-defined anywhere...

Pursuing a life of wonder can't happen under pressure. If you are looking at your watch every thirty seconds, the only thing you will wonder about is why God hasn't done anything in you yet...

Pursuing a life of wonder and participating in God's miracles—large and small... major and minor—requires the "carefree timelessness" to walk slowly and repeatedly around your "Jericho."

What is your "Jericho"?

Your "Jericho" might be—

- A recent doctor's diagnosis...
- A wayward child... parent... or spouse...
- An ethical dilemma at work...

Your "Jericho" might be—

- A service opportunity in your community...
- A mission adventure in a foreign land...

Your "Jericho" is whatever God has placed in your life that requires you to wait, wonder, and pray for "God's Glory" to shine forth as "God's Posture" stands tall.[2]

Pursuing a life of wonder and participating in the "Jericho" miracles God wants to do with and through you requires the "carefree timelessness" to wait. . . and repeat. . . and pray. . . and pause. . . and pursue. . . and trust. . . and pray. . . and. . .

"By faith, the Israelites marched around the walls of Jericho for seven days, and the walls fell flat" (Hebrews 11:30).

Chapter 15

Rahab: God's Inclusivity

I am not much of an art critic. My tastes, generally, run to velvet portraits of dogs shooting pool or playing poker. There are, however, a couple of masterworks that have captured my attention and imagination. One of them is Vincent Van Gogh's *Church at Auvers*.[1]

Toward the end of his life, his mental illnesses were overtaking him. In one, last burst of creative inspiration, Van Gogh painted over 100 paintings. Among them, he painted this church from a childhood memory.

As you enter the painting along the path in the foreground, there is light. Following the peasant woman along the path to the background, the church and sky seem to grow intimidatingly gloomy and dark. The church building, itself, has no clean, straight lines. It is distorted and seems to almost be quivering in the darkening shadows. The windows of the church are largely dark, but there are some vague hints of light inside.

Far from an inviting sanctuary and refuge, the church Van Gogh has painted is gloomy and foreboding and uninviting. Van Gogh's *Church at Auvers* appears spiritually dead.

Most disturbing, if you look carefully at the church building, it has no doors. This lack of doors is the most unsettling aspect of the painting. Among the questions this feature raises—

- Without doors, how can anyone enter the sanctuary of God's House?

- Does anyone inside the church care about those who are passing by outside?

Questions like these become important as Hebrews 11 shifts back to its roll-call of individuals living in faith relationships with "The Hero of Faithfulness," Almighty God.

The next individual highlighted in Hebrews 11 is one of the more questionable citizens in the list—"By faith the prostitute Rahab, because she welcomed the spies, was not killed with those who were disobedient" (Hebrews 11:31, NIV).

Rahab's problems are almost too numerous to detail—

- Rahab was a woman—strike one.
- Rahab was not an Israelite, she was a Canaanite, a citizen of Jericho—strike two.
- Rahab was also a prostitute—strike three.

Sarah and Moses' mother are the only other women mentioned in the listing of Hebrews 11. Certainly, the Old Testament contains more "upstanding" women in the vein of Proverbs 31 that the author of Hebrews could have chosen to include. Rachel, Rebekah, Ruth, Abigail, and Esther come quickly to mind.

But, under the inspiration of the Holy Spirit, it is "the prostitute Rahab" who is included in the roster of saints who have their faith applauded in this chapter. In spite of her impressive (?) collection of "strikes", Rahab helps us see an important piece of God's character. Rahab brings "God's Inclusivity" to the foreground.

Shortly after crossing the Red Sea, only two spies (Joshua and Caleb) had originally thought the Promised Land was conquerable. Now, forty years later, Joshua sends two more spies on an undercover mission to scope out the land.

Shortly before the Israelites crossed the Jordan River into the Promised Land, these two spies arrived in Jericho. With their cover almost blown, "Rahab the harlot" hid the spies from the authorities. After sending the town fathers on their way, Rahab rigged a basket out her window. She then lowered the spies to the ground and safety.

THE Hero of Faithfulness

In the process of helping them escape, Rahab said—

> I know that the Lord has given this land to you. . . . Now then, please swear to me by the Lord that you will show kindness to my family, because I have shown kindness to you. Give me a sure sign that you will spare the lives of my father and mother, my brothers and sisters, and all who belong to them, and that you will save us from death. . . (Joshua 2:9, 12-13, NIV).

After all the silent marches around the city, when the trumpets finally sounded and the people erupted with shouts, the walls of Jericho did come tumbling down. As promised, Rahab and her family were spared—"Joshua said to the two men who had spied out the land, 'Go into the prostitute's house and bring her out and all who belong to her, in accordance with your oath to her'" (Joshua 6:22, NIV).

Because she was faithful to the spies, Joshua and the Israelites kept their word by rescuing Rahab and her family from the midst of Jericho's destruction. Verse 23 says, "They brought out her entire family and put them in a place **outside the camp of Israel**" (Joshua 6:23, NIV, emphasis added).

Just two verses later, we read—"Joshua spared Rahab the prostitute, with her family and all who belonged to her, because she hid the men Joshua had sent as spies to Jericho—and she lives **among the Israelites to this day**" (Joshua 6:25, NIV, emphasis added).

In just these few verses, Rahab has made significant strides. First, she had to live "outside the camp." Then by the time the Book of Joshua was put down on scrolls for posterity, she and her family lived "among the Israelites." Bit by bit, Rahab is being included with God's Chosen People.

Even though the Bible is filled with genealogies, lists of names don't usually catch or hold our attention. We are much more likely to skip the Bible's impossible to pronounce names, than to study them at all. However, if we take the time to slog through all the names recorded in Matthew 1, we find the ultimate step in Rahab's inclusion with the nation of Israel.

Rahab: God's Inclusivity

Matthew's Genealogy of Jesus begins—

A record of the genealogy of Jesus Christ the son of David, the son of Abraham: Abraham was the father of Isaac, Isaac the father of Jacob, Jacob the father of Judah and his brothers, Judah the father of Perez and Zerah, whose mother was Tamar, Perez the father of Hezron, Hezron the father of Ram, Ram the father of Amminadab, Amminadab the father of Nahshon, Nahshon the father of Salmon, Salmon the father of Boaz, whose mother was Rahab, Boaz the father of Obed, whose mother was Ruth, Obed the father of Jesse, and Jesse the father of King David. David was the father of Solomon, whose mother had been Uriah's wife (Matthew 1:1-6, NIV).

As you were trying to figure out if that was a Hemi-powered Dodge Ram fathered by Hezron, did you catch who King David's Great-Great-Grandmother was?

- David's Dad—Jesse
- David's Grandpa—Obed
- David's Great-Grandpa—Boaz
- David's Great-Great-Grandpa—Salmon

And, Great-Great-Grandpa Salmon, we are told by Matthew, had a wife. Salmon's wife and Boaz's mother is Rahab. The very same prostitute saved from Jericho's destruction is a direct ancestor of Israel's greatest king—King David.

Talk about "God's Inclusivity!"

- Woman—strike one.
- Citizen of Canaan, not Israel—strike two.
- Prostitute—strike three.

Three strikes, but Rahab was not cast out! She was welcomed in!

Rahab should have died at Jericho. But she and her family were spared. Then she lived and dwelt among the Israelites. Within four generations, Rahab was included in the "house and lineage" of David.

By "God's Inclusivity," Rahab was made a direct ancestor of the Messiah, Jesus Christ! This can only happen because of the creative mercy of God.

Consider these minimum steps that had to have happened for Rahab to enter Jesus' lineage—

- Two spies had to take some initiative and show mercy to Rahab.
- Joshua had to acknowledge the spies' mercy and make sure to spare Rahab and her family.
- God had to honor these commitments and faithfully show His mercy to Rahab and to her descendants through the generations.

Keep the image of "the prostitute Rahab"—Jesus' direct, blood ancestor—in your mind as we return to the questions spawned by Van Gogh's *Church at Auvers*.

- Without doors, how can anyone enter the sanctuary of God's House?
- Does anyone inside the church care about those who are passing by outside?

It has repeatedly been said that the most segregated and exclusive time of the week in the United States of America is Sunday morning. The gatherings in most churches on Sunday mornings are far from the Bible's visions of all people and nations and tribes gathered together around heaven's throne. Instead, people who look alike, go to a church where everyone thinks alike, and they pray that no one unlike them in looks or thoughts will stumble into their midst.

A glance around your sanctuary on any given Sunday should raise some bright red flags—

- How inclusive is your church?
- Assuming your church has doors, are they locked or unlocked?
- How welcome would Rahab be in your church this Sunday?

It may sound harsh, but in many respects, the only organization more exclusive than the church in America today might be Augusta

Rahab: God's Inclusivity

National Golf Club—but even they just admitted their first two female members!

Is it any wonder people are not beating paths to churches and banging on church doors trying to get in?

In spite of our sinful ways, Hebrews 11 places a very inclusive God front and center—"By an act of faith, Rahab, the Jericho harlot, welcomed the spies and escaped the destruction that came on those who refused to trust God" (Hebrews 11:31).

In the musical group Casting Crowns' video to their song *Can Anybody Hear Her?* a young lady makes some sexual mistakes. Feeling the guilt of her Saturday night sin, she comes on Sunday morning to a church looking for something.

As she gets out of her car and straightens the dress she was wearing during the previous night's escapades, she is looked at disparagingly by one proper Christian lady. Self-conscious, but undeterred, she walks toward the church doors hoping to fit in with a group of her peers. But they never break stride as they rush past her. The girl's pain is palpable as she turns and walks away from the church.

The chorus to the song hauntingly wonders—

Does anybody hear her?
Can anybody see?
Or does anybody even know she's going down today
Under the shadow of our steeple
With all the lost and lonely people
Searching for the hope that's tucked away in you and me
Does anybody hear her?
Can anybody see?"[2]

This song begs for us to address some hard questions—

- Do we know what is going on in our communities, beyond the shadows of our church steeples?
- Are we just happy, plastic people playing hard at being nice as we hide behind our stained glass windows?
- Do we masquerade as Christians in our churches while remaining walled off from the world outside?

- Would a scarlet-letter bearing Rahab have a chance in a million at finding the true joy of Christ in our stained glass sanctuaries today?

Uncomfortable as these questions should make us, by the power of the Holy Spirit in Jesus' resurrection, we can live differently. Knowing the inclusive nature of God, we can lead a revolution in the church today.

2 Peter 3:9 declares—"The Lord is not slow in keeping His promise, as some understand slowness. He is patient with you, not wanting anyone to perish, but everyone to come to repentance" (2 Peter 3:9, NIV).

Sometimes we might wonder why God hasn't come back yet. We wonder why God doesn't just bring this evil world to an end. If pressed, we, reluctantly, acknowledge there is still outreach to be done.

Since we know Jesus, we would really prefer that Jesus just come back and get us to heaven—ASAP!

World saving is for others!

Dealing with scarlet-letter sinners is someone else's job!

However, God's deepest desire is that everyone comes to a saving knowledge of His grace. To this end, God the Father is patiently waiting for us to lead our friends and neighbors to His grace in His only-begotten Son, Jesus Christ.

God desires everyone—Jew and Gentile, slave and free, male and female (see Colossians 3:11)—to be included in the throngs and multitudes gathered forever in worship around His eternal throne. To bring this heavenly scene about, everyone who knows the grace of God in Jesus Christ has a role to play. It is our divinely-mandated job to work beyond "the shadows of our steeples," so lost and struggling people learn about grace and repentance and faith.

From Vincent Van Gogh to Casting Crowns, it doesn't take much to see that there is widespread rejection by many Christians of those not yet included in God's redeemed people. Time and time again, the church's doors are closed and locked and barred from the inside. The shadows of the church steeple can be among the loneliest places in the world.

Fortunately, God's faithfulness to Himself and His children can help us overcome our masquerading ways. God's faithfulness to Himself and to those Children who don't yet know Him can see us work for the good of the "Rahab's" in our midst.

Romans 12:1-2 says—

So here's what I want you to do, God helping you: Take your everyday, ordinary life—your sleeping, eating, going-to-work, and walking-around life—and place it before God as an offering. Embracing what God does for you is the best thing you can do for Him. Don't become so well-adjusted to your culture that you fit into it without even thinking. Instead, fix your attention on God. You'll be changed from the inside out. Readily recognize what He wants from you, and quickly respond to it. Unlike the culture around you, always dragging you down to its level of immaturity, God brings the best out of you, develops well-formed maturity in you (Romans 12:1-2).

The two spies Joshua sent into Jericho exemplify this type of "embracing what God does for you." God helped them take their "sleeping, eating, going-to-work, walking-around life" and pay attention to WHO they were brought in contact with.

With our attention focused on being transformed and used by God, and not succumbing to our culture, we can recognize AND respond to both the felt needs AND the spiritual needs of the people around us.

Later in Romans 12, Paul's encouragement and advice includes these charges—"Be alert servants of the Master, cheerfully expectant. . . Help needy Christians, be inventive in hospitality" (Romans 12:12-13).

Understanding that "God's Inclusiveness" extends to "the prostitute Rahab," as well as to the _____ [fill in the blank with words describing your sin] that you are, gives perspective to how God wants to use you to increase the population of persons gathered around His throne singing for eternity.

If Van Gogh's *Church at Auvers* represents the exclusive church, then visualize the all-inclusive scene John saw in Revelation 7. John—

. . .looked and there before me was a great multitude that no one could count, from every nation, tribe, people and language, standing before the throne and in front of the Lamb. They were wearing white robes and were holding palm branches in their hands. And they cried out in a loud voice: 'Salvation belongs to our God, who sits on the throne, and to the Lamb' (Revelation 7:9-10, NIV).

The multitude may not be countable, but it is made up of countless individuals. There are individuals included before the throne and the Lamb from EVERY people group on earth. They may appear faceless because they are so numerous, but each person surrounding God's throne has a name, a face, and a story. Each story is a testimony to "God's Inclusiveness."

I wonder. . .

If a survey were conducted in those crowds, how many stories from heaven's residents would include a reference to YOU?

How many people in heaven will credit your inventiveness at sharing the inclusiveness and hospitality of Jesus with their salvation story?

Interlude

"God's Sovereignty... Continues"

*C*onfession time—
One Sunday, I wasn't paying the closest attention to the preacher. Then he rattled off a quote that caught my ear. I never did get the source of the statement, but the quote is this—

- "The Bible knows nothing of solitary saints or spiritual hermits isolated from other believers and deprived of fellowship."

The great listing of patriarchs and saints in Hebrews 11 seems to agree. Recent chapters have shown Jacob in relationship with his grandsons. Joseph was restored to fellowship with his brothers. Moses returned from isolation in the desert to escape Egypt with over 600,000 fellow Israelites. Even Rahab, a non-Israelite, was made a part of the Hebrew nation following her rescue from Jericho.

The great social doctrines of American self-reliance and individualism attempt to argue in favor of "solitary saints" and "spiritual hermits." However, these American beliefs are flat-out wrong in God's eyes.

At this point in Hebrews 11, the author takes a pause before shifting into a final litany of saints and situations—"I could go on and on, but I've run out of time..." (Hebrews 11:32).

Put another way, the English Standard Version says—"And what more shall I say?" (Hebrews 11:32, ESV).

Back in verses 13-16, the writer of Hebrews paused to remind us about "God's Sovereignty" in the lives of His saints. This second brief pause in verse 32 reiterates the same theme—

- God is sovereign.
- God is sovereign OVER everything.
- God is sovereign IN everything.
- God is sovereign IN AND OVER our world and YOUR LIFE today.

We like talking about God's sovereignty, but we like to act as if we are fairly self-reliant. Sometimes we want to limit God's sovereignty to the lives and times of the biblical generations. Many times we allow the devil to con us into thinking God can't be strong enough, powerful enough, or present enough to exercise much, if any, sovereignty in our lives.

The author of Hebrews won't allow any of these flawed thoughts—"What more shall I say?"

Plenty, actually!

There are so many more—Gideon, Barak, Samson, Jephthah, David, Samuel, the prophets. . . . Through acts of faith, they toppled kingdoms, made justice work, took the promises for themselves. They were protected from lions, fires, and sword thrusts, turned disadvantage to advantage, won battles, routed alien armies. Women received their loved ones back from the dead. There were those who, under torture, refused to give in and go free, preferring something better: resurrection. Others braved abuse and whips, and, yes, chains and dungeons. We have stories of those who were stoned, sawed in two, murdered in cold blood; stories of vagrants wandering the earth in animal skins, homeless, friendless, powerless—the world didn't deserve them!—making their way as best they could on the cruel edges of the world (Hebrews 11:33-38).

Before continuing on with the study of Gideon, Barak, Samson, and the rest, we are going to pause for a refreshing look at "God's Sovereignty" in action today.

I grew up in Texas. Since I was actually born in Chicago to Upper Midwestern parents, I have been blessed to not have a Texas drawl. I do, however, regularly use two Texas, southern, redneck phrases in my speech.

The first is—"fixin' to. . ."

As in—

- "What are you doing?"
- "I'm fixin' to go to the store. . ."

Or—

- "Did you clean the cat box?"
- "I'm fixin' to. . ."

The second of my Texas, southern, redneck phrases is the ever-present—"Ya'll. . ."

As in—

- "What are ya'll doing?"
- "I'm fixin' to go to the store. . ."

Or—

- "Did ya'll clean the cat box?"
- "I'm fixin' to. . ."

"Fixin' to" covers every real or potential action a person might (or might not!) take.

"Ya'll" is the singular word for "you." (In case you were wondering, the plural of "ya'll" is—"all ya'll.")

Here comes the critical point to this little side trip down south. . .

God—in His sovereignty—is always "fixin' to" do something in "all ya'lls'" lives!

Even more personal—God is always "fixin' to" put "ya'll" into action on His behalf.

God is always "fixin' to" put YOU into action on His behalf!

In fact, God is so intent on getting you and me to go and serve Him, two-thirds of His Name is—"GO!"

Think about it. . .

Think about it some more. . .

Smile. . . groan. . .

Admit it. . . "ya'll" want to laugh—two-thirds of God's Name is GO!

Okay. . . now continue reading. . .

Every command God gives is really southern and redneck in nature—"Go. . . ya'll. . . cuz I'm fixin' to do a work through all ya'll!"

On several levels, these are important concepts to grasp. While these phrases may not prove God is a Texan, they could go a long way to proving God is at least a southern redneck! All ya'll know what I mean?

To show just how creative He can be in His sovereignty, one of the craziest works God did in the Bible is recorded in Mark 5.

After being awakened from a much-needed nap in the back of the boat and calming the wind and waves at the end of Mark 4, Jesus and His disciples landed on the other side of the Sea of Galilee.

As Jesus got out of the boat, a psycho madman came up to Him. This lunatic terrorized the community. He even terrorized the cemetery. The graves of the community's ancestors weren't safe from this nut. No chains could bind him. In general, this demon-possessed whack job made life miserable for everyone. In all regards, this dude was an unholy terror.

When the crazed madman began to verbally assault Jesus, Jesus calmly asked the demons inside the man their names. Knowing Jesus was about to cast them out of the man, the demons inside begged Jesus to have mercy on them and allow them to remain in the country.

Let Scripture continue the narrative—"A large herd of pigs was browsing and rooting on a nearby hill. The demons begged Him, 'Send us to the pigs so we can live in them.' Jesus gave the order. But it was even worse for the pigs than for the man. Crazed, they stampeded over a cliff into the sea and drowned" (Mark 5:11-13).

Jesus' Jewish disciples were probably (secretly!) thrilled to see all that unclean pork go plunging over the cliffs to a watery grave.

The locals, however, were pretty upset. That herd of swine was their livelihood. Those pigs were their source of income. Those hogs also were the supply of animals for the sacrifices they made to their local gods.

Once they overcame their awe and shock at what had happened, the pig-herders demanded that Jesus leave the area.

> As Jesus was getting into the boat, the demon-delivered man begged to go along, but [Jesus] wouldn't let him. Jesus said, 'Go home to your own people. Tell them your story—what the Master did, how He had mercy on you.' The man went back and began to preach in the Ten Towns area about what Jesus had done for him. He was the talk of the town (Mark 5:18-20).

Did you hear what Jesus just did?

For starters, the healing of the cemetery-dwelling, demon-possessed psycho was incredible. The pig stampede off the cliffs was also pretty impressive. However, the most shocking part of the event was Jesus' rejection of the man as a disciple.

Take a couple minutes. . . and read Mark 4:18-20, again—

> As Jesus was getting into the boat, the demon-delivered man begged to go along, but [Jesus] wouldn't let him. Jesus said, 'Go home to your own people. Tell them your story—what the Master did, how He had mercy on you.' The man went back and began to preach in the Ten Towns area about what Jesus had done for him. He was the talk of the town (Mark 5:18-20).

Jesus did not enroll the former madman into a 16-week (at least!) instruction class focusing on church membership and all the fine points of Christian doctrine that cause division between one denomination and the next. Nor did Jesus hand the man an application form to a four year Bible college or seminary.

What Jesus did is so shocking, you might need to read Mark 4:18-20, yet again—

> As Jesus was getting into the boat, the demon-delivered man begged to go along, but [Jesus] wouldn't let him. Jesus said, 'Go home to your own people. Tell them your story—what the Master did, how He had mercy on you.' The man went back and began to preach in the Ten Towns area about what Jesus had done for him. He was the talk of the town (Mark 5:18-20).

Jesus immediately sent the man as a missionary to his people in the region!

The "Gerasene Demoniac," as he is known, went from psycho to sent in one afternoon!

He went from madman to missionary in just a few moments!

This man was at one minute demon-possessed and in the next moment, divinely sent by Jesus to evangelize ten different cities!

Come again?

As crazy as it sounds, Jesus would not let him travel back to Galilee with Him. Rather, Jesus' charge to him was—"Tell them your story!"

Crazy it may be, but this is the same charge Jesus still gives today. Under God's sovereignty, we are to—

- TELL OUR story of what God has done in us!
- LIVE OUR story of what God is doing in us!

Because—

- God is FIXIN' to do something through each of YA'LL!!

Trust me when I say—I understand your squeamishness at Jesus' command! I don't like talking about myself. I am certain no one wants to know what is going on in my life. Besides, most of the time, I'm not even sure anything spiritual or worthwhile is happening in my life!

WRONG!

You are wrong and so am I!

If God is present, God is active!

More—SINCE God is present, God is at work!

"Go home to your own people. **Tell them your story**—what the Master did, how He had mercy on you" (Mark 5:19, emphasis added).

You don't need a "Psycho-to-Sent"... "Madman-to-Missionary"... "Dragged-Out-of-the-Gutter-into-the-Pulpit" story like the demon-possessed man in Mark 5.

All you need is trust that since God lives in you, He is worth talking about to other people.

Martin Luther addressed how to do this by telling a cobbler to interact with his customers by making a good pair of shoes and selling them at a fair price. Knowing this, and living this way, would bring glory to God!

In other words—

- Be WHO you are...
- WHERE you are...
- With WHAT you have...

Because—

- God is FIXIN' to do a great work in and through YA'LL!

Extraordinary circumstances provide memorable stories that help us realize God's sovereignty. Even more than the extraordinary, however, it is ordinary daily life that provides the backdrop against which God's sovereignty plays out in our lives.

To see God's sovereignty at work, look at the life of Gladys Aylward, a simple English parlor maid. Once Gladys received God's grace in Jesus Christ, she dreamed of going to another country to share Jesus with others.

In the early 1930s, Gladys applied to become a missionary with the China Inland Mission. However, she failed to meet their entrance requirements. Undeterred, she bought a train ticket and—with no support or plan—she set out across Russia on the Trans-Siberian Railway.

Eventually, Gladys settled in a remote province of China. Joining another missionary she met there, they opened an inn for mule drivers. As the men enjoyed good food and a warm bed, they also were entertained with stories of Jesus.

Sometime later, Chinese officials commissioned Gladys to help abolish the ancient custom of foot-binding. Under "God's

Sovereignty," the one-time English parlor maid had access to Chinese homes and undreamed-of opportunities to spread the Good News of Jesus Christ.

Through the years, Gladys also became involved in prison reform. She established orphanages, leper treatment centers, and churches. Simple, average, regular, British parlor maid Gladys Aylward served the Chinese people until her death in 1970.

Speaking about her life, Gladys Aylward said—"My heart is full of praise that one so insignificant, uneducated, and ordinary in every way could be used to His glory for the blessing of His people in poor persecuted China."[1]

Do you believe you are too insignificant to tell people about Jesus—ya'll are NOT!

Do you think you are not educated enough to be a witness for Jesus—ya'll are NOT!

Do you believe you are too ordinary to have an extraordinary impact for God's Kingdom—ya'll are NOT!

You have been called, equipped, empowered, and sent by the "God of GO!"

The only question left is—

- Since God is sovereign and His Holy Spirit resides in you giving you all the help and hope you need. . . what are you going to attempt in His Name?

Or, as our southern, redneck God would put it—

- Since I AM with YA'LL, what are YA'LL FIXIN' to do?

Chapter 16

"Gideon: God's Vulnerability"

"*I* could go on and on, but I've run out of time. There are so many more. . ." (Hebrews 11:32).

Transitioning from one portion of Hebrews 11 to the next, the author of Hebrews quickly rattles off a list of six names. It is almost as if the writer is trying to prove "how many more" Old Testament persons there are to talk about—"Gideon, Barak, Samson, Jephthah, David, Samuel. . ."

Through the first thirty-one verses of Hebrews 11, each person or event named has taken us on a chronological faith-journey through Scripture. From Creation through the fall of Jericho, each relationship with the "Hero of Faithfulness" has followed the timeline of history from Genesis to Exodus to Joshua.

With many more topics to cover, the author of Hebrews throws the chronological sequence out the window.

Gideon is named before Barak. But Barak's tale is told in Judges 4. Gideon's in Judges 6-7.

Samson (see Judges 16-17) is listed before Jephthah (see Judges 11-12).

David beginning in 1 Samuel 16-17, among volumes more, is named before Samuel (see 1 Samuel 3 and following).

- Is this just random?
- Did the author, in his haste to complete his letter and get these important words circulating, just get a few names out of order?
- Or is the writer of Hebrews trying to make a point?

I'm of the opinion that there is no misplaced pronoun or wasted word in Scripture. I believe every jot and tittle has been inspired by the Holy Spirit and freely written by the men and women "God spoke to. . . at many times and in various ways" (Hebrews 1:1, NIV). If I am correct in this assessment, then the inversion of these names must mean something.

Over the next several chapters, we are going to look at the order in which these six names are listed. We are going to approach them as three sets of two person pairs. With each couple displaying two important attributes of "The Hero of Faithfulness."

As we turn our attention to the first couple, Gideon and Barak, theologian, author, and pastor, Leonard Sweet, raises a challengingly brilliant question—

We love to sing the Jack Hayford song 'Majesty.' We love to sing about our 'Awesome God.' But when was the last time you sang about God's vulnerability, God's woundedness? What sets apart the Christian God from all other gods is not how majestic and awesome God is but how vulnerable and wounded God became for our sakes.[1]

Pause.
Stop.
Center yourself.
Re-read these words—"What sets apart the Christian God from all other gods is not how majestic and awesome God is but how vulnerable and wounded God became for our sakes."

Now take a minute to honestly reflect over your recent worship experiences.

We sing frequently about OUR woundedness and vulnerabilities, but—

- When WAS the last time you sang about GOD'S vulnerability?
- When WAS the last time you sang about GOD's woundedness?
- For that matter, have you ever considered how vulnerable and wounded GOD is?

We are much more likely to sing and pray to an "Awesome God" who is "Indescribable," than to a vulnerable God.

We are much more comfortable worshiping a "God of Wonders" and "Majesty," than a wounded God.

Each year, near Easter, we take time to read Isaiah's Messianic prophecies about "The Suffering Servant"—

> He had no beauty or majesty to attract us to Him, nothing in His appearance that we should desire Him. He was despised and rejected by men, a man of sorrows, and familiar with suffering. Like one from whom men hide their faces He was despised, and we esteemed Him not. Surely He took up our infirmities and carried our sorrows, yet we considered Him stricken by God, smitten by Him, and afflicted (Isaiah 53:2b-4, NIV).

Even on the rare occasion when we do acknowledge the woundedness of Christ, we prefer to limit any vulnerabilities within the Triune God as a whole, to Jesus Christ, the 2nd Person part.

We are comfortable singing about an "Awesome God" and we are drawn to the "Majesty" of God because this God is an otherworldly God. This God of majesty and awesomeness transcends and rises above all the issues of sin and slovenliness that this world—and our sinful selves, in particular—wallows in.

That God is transcendent is absolutely true! That God is above and beyond this world of sin and shame is beyond debate. That God is wholly holy and seated firmly on heaven's throne is a large portion of what makes Him God.

Read Isaiah 6. No other conclusion can be drawn than that the Triune God of Isaiah's vision transcends lowly earthliness—

> In the year that King Uzziah died, I saw the Lord sitting on a throne, high and lifted up, and the train of His *robe* filled the temple. Above it stood seraphim; each one had six wings: with two he covered his face, with two he covered his feet, and with two he flew. And one cried to another and said: 'Holy, holy, holy *is* the Lord of hosts; The whole earth *is* full of His glory!' And the posts of the door were shaken by the voice

of him who cried out, and the house was filled with smoke (Isaiah 6:1-4, NKJV, italics in original).

As transcendent as He is, however, the God of the Bible is not merely above and beyond. What sets Him apart (among other things!) from all other false gods is that He is also immanent. God is also close to us. God is also the God nearby. The God of the Bible is the God who "when the time had fully come... sent His Son, born of a woman, born under law, to redeem those under law, that we might receive the full rights of sons" (Galatians 4:4-5, NIV).

Talk about vulnerable!

- Choosing to leave heaven... for earth!
- Adding humanity... to the divine!
- Submitting to the confines of the Law... when He was the Author of the Law!

Perhaps no individual in Hebrews 11's litany give us a better perspective into "God's Vulnerability" than Gideon. The relationship between God and Gideon begins in Judges 6:11—

One day the angel of God came and sat down under the oak in Ophrah that belonged to Joash the Abiezrite, whose son Gideon was threshing wheat in the winepress, out of sight of the Midianites. The angel of God appeared to him and said, 'God is with you, O mighty warrior!' (Judges 6:11-12).

To say Gideon isn't overly excited by God's call to go fight the Midianites would be an understatement. Gideon's underwhelming responses to God can be summarized as—

- "Who... me?!"
- "Who... me... I'm from Manasseh... and we are pitiful!?"
- "Who... me... I'm the weakest person in this whole pitiful tribe?!"
- "Who... me... are you crazy God!?"

"Gideon: God's Vulnerability"

With no hint that He is rethinking His selection of Gideon, God takes all the excuses and cuts to the quick—"I'll be with you. Believe Me, you'll defeat Midian as one man" (Judges 6:16).

Even with God's pledge—"I AM with you!"—Gideon hesitates. Gideon remains reluctant. Gideon wants a sign from God that this battle against Midian will really be successful.

God obliges Gideon's request for a sign. God tells Gideon to BBQ a young goat and fix up a bushel of flatbread. Just before ringing the dinner bell, Gideon soaks the whole meal in gravy.

Then—"The angel of God stretched out the tip of the stick he was holding and touched the meat and the bread. Fire broke out of the rock and burned up the meat and bread while the angel of God slipped away out of sight" (Judges 6:21-22).

Gideon was rightly impressed by this divine display. But still he was not entirely convinced. Only after demanding a few more displays of God's power, did Gideon relent and acknowledge God's calling on his life.

Finally, Gideon obediently raises an army to battle the Midianites. The only problem? When he finally takes action, Gideon raises an army that God deems too large for the fight. God decides too many Israelite men have responded to Gideon's battle call. God tells Gideon anyone feeling the slightest bit queasy about attacking the Midianites can go home. Over two-thirds of the army can't stomach the fight, so they leave.

Still, the remaining army is too large for God's purposes. Down at the river, God sorts the men again. This time only 300 men survive God's "How-to-Drink-from-the-River" test.

300!

Let's tick off just a few of the vulnerabilities God is showing—

- Choosing Gideon. . . from the weakest tribe among all of His Chosen People. . .
- Sending two-thirds of the army home. . .
- Releasing almost all the rest of the army. . .
- Keeping only 300 men to fight Midian. . .
- Oh. . . and those 300 men left to do battle? They were not trained military men like the soldiers in Midian's army. . .

As if all this weren't enough, pay close attention to how God arms Gideon's 300 men for the battle—"[God] divided the three hundred men into three companies. He gave each man a trumpet and an empty jar, with a torch in the jar" (Judges 7:16).

Are you kidding me?

Where are the swords and battle axes? How about a few chariots and some archers?

Who fights battles against vastly superior enemies with trumpets, jars, and torches?

Just the most vulnerable God in all of history, that's who!

Several years ago, I taught a comparative religion class at our local community college. In the reading and preparation I did for that class, I can recall no other god who displays any vulnerability, let alone such complete vulnerability.

- Mohammed—always powerful and completely distant.
- Buddha—always mysterious and unreachable.
- Hinduism's countless millions of gods—anything and everything, but never weak or vulnerable.
- Animistic gods—always winning battles and conquering enemies through fear.

Think of the myths about Greek and Roman gods. These gods occasionally lowered themselves to mingle among humans. However, their interactions with humans were always in displays of strength and power and dominance.

Only "The Hero of Faithfulness" exposes Himself to the vulnerabilities, weaknesses, and frailties of human life. Only "The Hero of Faithfulness" becomes fully human, yet remains fully God. Only "The Hero of Faithfulness" attempts what Paul describes in Philippians 2—

> Christ Jesus. . . being in very nature God, did not consider equality with God something to be grasped, but made Himself nothing, taking the very nature of a servant, being made in human likeness. And being found in appearance as a man, He humbled Himself and became obedient to death—even death on a cross! (Philippians 2:5-8, NIV).

This humble, obedient, servant God is the vulnerable God on display in Gideon's life. This vulnerable God is the One we see at work when Gideon battles the Midianites.

Here, then, is our challenge—

- If God is willing to make Himself vulnerable, why do we go to such great lengths to put on such pitiful acts of strength?

God puts Himself and His reputation on the line to save us from sin, death, the devil, and our own self through some pretty risky and vulnerable means. Yet we are always trying to make ourselves more than, or at least, other than, we really are.

Repeatedly, God tells us—

- "Whoever welcomes this little child in My name welcomes Me; and whoever welcomes Me welcomes the one who sent Me. For he who is least among you all—he is the greatest" (Luke 9:48, NIV).
- "So the last will be first, and the first will be last" (Matthew 20:16, NIV).

But we struggle (at best!) to accept God's least and last concept. For that matter, so did Gideon.

After routing the Midianites with his measly 300 men blowing their trumpets, breaking their jars, and shining their torches, Gideon struggled to maintain his humility. Following his battles, the warrior from the weakest clan in the most pitiful tribe wanted some recognition. Gideon felt he had earned some spoils from the battle. So Gideon solicited all the golden earrings from the plunder taken from the Midianites.

Golden earrings might not sound like much, but—"the gold earrings that Gideon had asked for weighed about forty-three pounds—and that didn't include the crescents and pendants, the purple robes worn by the Midianite kings, and the ornaments hung around the necks of their camels" (Judges 8:25-26).

Around 1200-1300 BC, gold prices may not have been over $1600 an ounce, as they are today. Regardless, for a guy used to threshing wheat in a winepress, Gideon was making himself a wealthy, wealthy man.

Fast-forward from Gideon's to Jesus' generation and nothing had changed. Even with the humble, obedient, servant Messiah leading them around Israel, Jesus' disciples regularly tried to grab gusto and power. Peter, James, John, and the boys fought more than once over how to best organize themselves in Jesus' presence. None of Jesus' chosen Twelve wanted to be least or last. They all wanted to be first and foremost.

In our quest to be more than, greater than, or other than, who we are, it is vital that we remember WHOSE we are. We need to stay focused on WHAT it means to belong to God the Father through the grace of God the Son.

As we sing about the "Majesty" of our "Awesome God," we need to remember the nearness and vulnerability of God. He is in our midst. He is close to us. He is Immanuel—"God-with-us."

Set aside all the "White Christmas" Bing Crosby inspired nostalgia. Turn off the blinking LED lights. Look past the holly decked halls. Clearly think that last phrase through—

- Immanuel—"God-with-us"

Leonard Sweet tells a story that helps us understand "God's Vulnerability" at being Immanuel—"God-with-us."

Disclaimer: at first, this story is going to seem strange!

Fair warning: prepare yourself now to read these next paragraphs at least twice!

> A man was so worried he was on the verge of a nervous breakdown that he decided to see a psychiatrist. 'What's your problem?' the psychiatrist asked. 'Actually, I've got two problems,' the man replied. 'My first problem is that I don't think I'm human anymore. I'm starting to think I'm a soft-drink vending machine, and I can dispense six different kinds of soda for a dollar each: orange, grape, lime, cherry, birch beer, and Coke.'

"Gideon: God's Vulnerability"

The doctor pondered the man's calm demeanor for a while, then decided on a course of action. He got out four quarters and said to the man: 'Open your mouth. I'll have a birch beer, please.'

Whereupon the man answered: 'That's my second problem: I'm out of order.'[2]

I warned you the story was going to seem strange.
Did you read it a second time?
Here are the points—
First, whatever you think you are (and, hopefully you don't think you are a vending machine!), we frequently forget WHOSE we are. Whatever else you might be, you are a sinner chosen by God. You have been united with Christ by His divine grace and unending mercy.

"God's Vulnerability" led Him to call us to Himself. "God's Vulnerability" led Him to join us to Himself—

> . . .not because of righteous things we had done, but because of His mercy. He saved us through the washing of rebirth and renewal by the Holy Spirit, whom He poured out on us generously through Jesus Christ our Savior, so that, having been justified by His grace, we might become heirs having the hope of eternal life (Titus 3:4-7, NIV).

You belong to Christ!
You are in relationship with the God of the universe!
You are a child belonging to "The Hero of Faithfulness"!
This serves, then, to expose our second problem. Because we forget our relationship to Jesus Christ is based on His choosing us— we are "Out of Order."
We want to be first, not last.
We want to be greatest, not least.
We want strength, not weakness.
With logic that defies and far surpasses all human comprehension, God—who has made us His own—calls us to be last. God tells us to

be least. God declares our weakness is the perfect platform for His strength to be displayed upon.

Gideon's first response to God was probably his best—"Gideon said to Him, '*Me*, my master? How and with what could I ever save Israel? Look at me. My clan's the weakest in Manasseh and I'm the runt of the litter.' God said to him, 'I'll be with you. Believe Me, you'll defeat Midian as one man'" (Judges 6:15-16, italics in original).

Perfect in weakness!

Perfect in "runt-ness"!

Perfect because I AM is with us!

Perfect because we have a God willing to humble Himself and become vulnerable—"even to death on the cross."

Chapter 17

"Barak: God's Position"

*A*re you ready for a revolutionary thought? God does NOT call us to be leaders!

You CANNOT find one instance in the Bible of God saying—"Lead Me. . ."

You CAN find statements all throughout God's Word of Jesus saying—"Follow Me. . ."

Here are just a few examples—

- "'Come, follow Me,' Jesus said, 'and I will make you fishers of men.' At once they left their nets and followed Him. . ." (Matthew 4:19-20, NIV).
- "As [Jesus] walked along, He saw Levi son of Alphaeus sitting at the tax collector's booth. 'Follow Me,' Jesus told him, and Levi got up and followed Him. . ." (Mark 2:14, NIV).
- "Jesus answered, 'If I want him to remain alive until I return, what is that to you? You must follow Me. . .'" (John 21:22, NIV).

In spite of everything our culture and churches teach us—

- God DOES NOT call us to be leaders!
- God DOES call us to be followers!

THE Hero of Faithfulness

One of the most critical questions for every person living in relationship with Jesus Christ by the power of the Holy Spirit to address is—

- Are you ready to be a follower?

Which, honestly, just doesn't sound like much fun.
Following doesn't sound glamorous. Leading sounds important.
Following sounds weak. Leading sounds like strength.
Following seems to imply something is lacking. Leading seems to be where power and control reside.
Leading and following. . .
Following and leading. . .

As we turn to the second partner in Hebrews 11:32's first pair, leading and following—or, following and leading—reside in a very dynamic tension. From this tension, the relationship between Gideon and Barak develops the relationship between "God's Vulnerability" and "God's Position."

Raise your hand if you know Barak's story?

I'm asking about the Barak of the Bible, not the Barack who resides at 1600 Pennsylvania Avenue, in Washington, D.C.

The name is the same. While virtually everyone has heard of Barack Obama, very few know anything about the Barak of the Bible.

Of all the people listed in Hebrews 11, Barak is not the 44th President of the United States. Neither is Barak the "Father of Many Nations" like Abraham. Barak also did not save the world from a devastating famine like Joseph. He didn't go face to face with the Pharaoh of Egypt until the Israelites were freed like Moses. As a matter of fact, Hebrews 11's Barak is not even the primary player in his own story.

The Book of Judges records the roller coaster history of Israel. The couple hundred years covered by the Book of Judges sees a vicious cycle of ups and downs and twists and turns that repeats itself over and over.

First, the people of Israel do evil in God's sight. As a result, God allows an enemy nation to oppress them. Eventually, the Children of Israel cry out for God's help. In His time, God raises up a judge to redeem the people. Peace exists throughout the land for a number of years. But sin once again rears its ugly head and the people return to doing evil in God's sight. With this, the roller coaster makes another stomach-churning loop through the circuit.

In Judges 4 and 5, the evil in the Israelite nation leads to oppression at the hands of the Canaanites. King Jabin and Sisera, commander of the Canaanite army, run roughshod over Israel for twenty years.

During this time, a female prophet named Deborah, from the tribe of Ephraim, was rendering decisions in Israel. Over time, the oppression throughout the land grew worse. For a reason Scripture doesn't reveal, Deborah sends for Barak.

When Barak arrived in the land of Ephraim, from his home in the land of Naphtali, Deborah told him—

> The Lord, the God of Israel, commands you: 'Go, take with you ten thousand men of Naphtali and Zebulun and lead the way to Mount Tabor. I will lure Sisera, the commander of Jabin's army, with his chariots and his troops to the Kishon River and give him into your hands' (Judges 4:6-7, NIV).

As he steps from the background to the foreground for his moment of glory, Barak responds somewhat timidly to Deborah's words—"If you go with me, I will go; but if you don't go with me, I won't go" (Judges 4:8, NIV).

Barak of the Bible hardly leaps onto Scripture's stage with the confidence and boldness of a junior Senator from Illinois. Instead of being a natural-born leader, it almost appears Barak is a coward, afraid to do battle with Sisera.

Usually, Barak is disparaged for not grabbing the proverbial bull by the horns and charging gung-ho into battle against the Canaanites. Normally, equal amounts of blame and shame are heaped on Barak for his refusal to do the manly thing and lead the army into battle alone.

In all honesty, however, a cowardly Barak might reveal some real intelligence on his part. Among other weapons and warriors, Sisera has 900 iron chariots at his disposal. Israel, on the far and distant other end of the military spectrum, has a ragtag, all-volunteer army of ill-equipped farmers and plowmen.

Barak's timidity might disguise some real genius. It is possible Barak recognizes Deborah is the prophetess and judge of Israel. Having been summoned form his humble home by the lady leading Israel, it is possible Barak recognizes that Deborah is the person whom God has selected for the nation's leadership.

Here is one hugely counterintuitive piece to Barak's story. Deborah is the Judge. Deborah is the prophetess. Deborah is the national leader. Yet because he followed Deborah, Barak—not Deborah—is listed in Hebrews 11. Not only that, there is no mention made in Hebrews 11 of Jael, the lady whose courage and quick-thinking drove a tent peg through Sisera's temple (see Judges 4:21), truly rescuing Israel from the Canaanite menace.

One accusation made by some of those who believe a misogynistic Paul wrote the Book of Hebrews is that Barak is included and Deborah and Jael are excluded from Hebrews 11 in some kind of "put-the-women-in-their-place" omission. However, the fact that Rahab and Moses' mother are spoken of earlier in the litany of Hebrews 11 mitigates against the omission of Deborah and Jael because they were women.

Listen closely to Deborah's response to Barak's request for her to come with him—"Very well. . . I will go with you. But because of the way you are going about this, the honor will not be yours, for the Lord will hand Sisera over to a woman" (Judges 4:9-10, NIV).

Barak wants to follow. Glory does not interest him. Credit is not important to him. Barak is content working alongside—even behind—a woman, especially when that woman is God's chosen leader of the nation.

Here's the nutshell—

Gideon put "God's Vulnerability" on display. Barak builds on that by putting "God's Position" on display.

The question for us to wrestle with is—

- "God's Position" is as The Leader. . . are you ready to follow?

It doesn't take a genius to conclude that this early 21st century generation is consumed with all aspects of leadership. A quick search of the word "leadership" in Amazon books brings 107,988 results (I'm sure if you run the same search now, the number will be even greater!).

The same search for the word "followership" only registers 227 results (and I was surprised there were that many!).

The leadership craze is not just an American cultural beast trying to help secular people build their businesses and relationships. When it comes to the quest to develop the best leaders, the American Christian church is virtually indistinguishable from culture.

Leadership opportunities are being maximized in countless biblical principles, numerous irrefutable laws, and list upon list of easy-to-manage steps. The opportunities to learn leadership ("all for the low, low price of...") in innumerable workshops, conventions, and books, are everywhere.

The church's overwhelming leadership search is aimed at raising up the next generation of great church leaders. Which, on its face, is absurd because raising up "great leaders"—or even lousy leaders, for that matter!—is the Holy Spirit's job!

In some manner or fashion, "3 B's" dominate most church leadership conversations—

- Butts—how many of them are filling your pews?
- Buildings—how is your fundraising campaign to erect the next, bigger one going?
- Benjamins—how much money do you have in the bank?

The vast majority of these leadership initiatives in the church boil down to the same "ABC's"—

- A is for Attendance...
- B is for Buildings...
- C is for Cash...
- D is for Deliverables...
- E is for Ego...
- F is for Faustian deal...

What?

"F" is for—what?

According to a German legend, Faust was a highly successful, but unfortunately discontent, scholar who made a pact with the devil. Faust exchanged his soul for unlimited knowledge and worldly pleasures. A "Faustian deal" is one in which moral integrity is surrendered in order to achieve power and success.

Applied to the "ABCs of Church Leadership," in a "Faustian deal" moral (or should I say, biblical?) integrity is proverbially "sold to the devil" for some kind of ongoing glory. The constant pursuit of these deliverable and measurable statistics (butts. . . buildings. . . and Benjamins) often leads church leaders into a "devil's contract."

Jesus summarized this "Faustian" choice in Matthew's Gospel—"No one can serve two masters; for either he will hate the one and love the other, or else he will be loyal to the one and despise the other. You cannot serve God and mammon" (Matthew 6:24, NKJV).

When put this way—God or mammon—we all recoil and quickly mouth that we follow God. We will always follow God. We would never not follow God. Too doubt, wonder, or question this is tantamount to sacrilege. Irrespective of what our lips piously proclaim, mammon doesn't give up so easily. Neither does the devil.

The "Faustian" choice is almost never conscious. But such devilishly-detailed choices are located in the slime coating the slippery slope of leadership. Maintaining status as a "real church leader" is always predicated on more and more and more attendance, buildings, and cash. More than one scandal in the Christian Church over the past couple decades has revealed how proficient we are at packaging the details of our bedeviling choices into acceptable "church-speak."

Yet Barak shows us a different way—"If you go with me, I will go; but if you don't go with me, I won't go" (Judges 4:8, NIV).

As you consider Barak's inclusion in Hebrews 11, make sure to not miss this critical point about following— following still requires action.

Barak did not shirk the staggering responsibility Deborah had given him. Barak still was at the front of the battle when 10,000 overmatched Israelite men battled against Sisera and the vastly superior Canaanite army. Barak followed, all the while, making sure Deborah—God's chosen Judge of Israel—was in position so she could continue to relay God's Word along the way.

In many and various ways, leaders want their ego massaged and stroked.

Simply, followers want God to be glorified.

Leaders believe success (and some measure of eternal reward) is measured by their position at the head of the line.

Followers realize success is solely measured by "God's Position."

Followers understand success is not found by where your name is displayed on the company's letterhead. Followers know success is not measured by how many listings pop up when you Google yourself. For that matter, real followers probably don't know how to Google themselves!

Success—especially, spiritual success—is measured by "God's Position." Success is a tenor and tone that knows how to relate to others. Success is part of the make-up and mind-set of those comfortable with themselves because of who they are IN Christ Jesus.

Perhaps the greatest example of leadership and followership is found in John 13. As Jesus and His disciples gathered in the Upper Room on the night Jesus was betrayed, if anyone should have been positioned at the head of the table, it was Jesus. In yet another display of vulnerability, Jesus overlooks a major error by the event planners.

Instead of demanding His rightful position at the head of everything—including the line of those getting a foot massage by a lowly slave—Jesus got up "from the supper table, set aside His robe, and put on an apron. Then He poured water into a basin and began to wash the feet of the disciples, drying them with His apron" (John 13:4-5).

Instead of making excuses or placing blame for the lack of amenities at the Last Supper, Jesus shows vulnerability, when He serves His disciples—

> Do you understand what I have done to you? You address me as 'Teacher' and 'Master,' and rightly so. That is what I am. So if I, the Master and Teacher, washed your feet, you must now wash each other's feet. I've laid down a pattern for you. What I've done, you do. I'm only pointing out the obvious. A servant is not ranked above his master; an employee doesn't give orders to the employer. If you understand what I'm telling you, act like it—and live a blessed life (John 13:12-17).

In the Upper Room, before dinner and before instituting Holy Communion, Jesus establishes a pattern for service. Like usual, the disciples weren't sure how to understand (let alone, apply!) what Jesus had just done. As time went by, however, service—both within and outside the family of God— became an integral part of how to follow Jesus.

Very quickly, in Acts 6, the early church faced an issue over how to make sure all the widows were properly taken care of. After prayer and fasting, it was agreed to designate seven men to be deacons. Their job was to help organize the human care ministries of the early church. One of the deacons chosen was Philip.

In Acts 8, Philip famously follows the lead of the Holy Spirit outside town, to a chariot parked on the side of the road. Because he followed the Holy Spirit's prompting, Philip is instrumental in bringing an Ethiopian eunuch to faith in Jesus Christ.

This event is just about the last time we hear of Philip in Scripture. However, extra-biblical documents tell about a lifetime of faithful service Philip rendered to God and the community in Caesarea.

For the rest of his long life, Philip served one church congregation with great humility. According to tradition, Philip spent hours and hours and hours on his knees in prayer. Philip spent so much time on his knees that he developed thick, camel-like callouses on them. To those in the early church, Philip became known as "Old Camel Knees."

Following "God's Position" is all about humility and vulnerability. Philip humbled himself through a lifetime of prayer. Barak allowed himself to become vulnerable when he followed Deborah. The Canaanites were vanquished and peace reigned throughout Israel for the rest of Barak's life.

In a great celebration of "God's Position," following the defeat of the Canaanites, Barak and Deborah sang—

> When they let down their hair in Israel, they let it blow wild in the wind. The people volunteered with abandon, bless God! Hear O kings! Listen O princes! To God, yes, to God, I'll sing, Make music to God, to the God of Israel. God, when you left Seir, marched across the fields of Edom, Earth quaked, yes, the skies poured rain, oh, the clouds made rivers. Mountains

leapt before God, the Sinai God, before God, the God of Israel (Judges 5:2-5).

What do you think?
Are you ready to be a follower?

Chapter 18

"Samson: God's Strength"

 little quiz to get the brain cells firing...

- My DNA absorbed radiation from the yellow star around which Earth orbits. This radiation interacted with the radiation I already possessed from my original red star. Which superhero am I?
- Unlike other superheroes, I have no super powers. Following the murder of my parents, I trained myself physically and intellectually to overcome evil by out-thinking criminals and bringing them to justice. Which superhero am I?
- While on a school fieldtrip, I was bit by a radioactive animal. From this animal bite, I received the superpowers of strength, agility, balance, and speed. Which superhero am I?

In order, the correct answers are—

- Superman
- Batman
- Spiderman

Just for fun, here is one more superhero question—

- "A razor has never touched my head. I've been God's Nazirite from conception. If I were shaved, my strength would leave me; I would be as helpless as any other mortal" (Judges 16:17). Which superhero am I?

Trick question!

The correct answer is Samson. But Samson is no superhero. Superman, Batman, and Spiderman are three fictional, comic book and action movie creations of the human imagination. Samson is the real-life, flesh-and-blood judge of Israel ordained by God to rescue the nation from the oppression of the Philistines. Samson is the next sinful human being listed in Hebrews 11. Samson is the next person the author of Hebrews lists to show the faithfulness and character of God to His people.

Judges 12 ends with a series of brief statements concerning three rapid-succession judges of Israel. With virtually no details, Ibzan, Elon, and Abdon ruled Israel for a total of twenty-five years.

Judges 13, then, begins this tale—"The People of Israel were back at it again, doing what was evil in God's sight. God put them under the domination of the Philistines for forty years" (Judges 13:1).

To release the Israelites from the oppression of the Philistines, God sends His angel to a childless couple living in the northern Israelite territory of Dan. The angel appeared and said—

> I know that you are barren and childless, but you're going to become pregnant and bear a son. But take much care: Drink no wine or beer; eat nothing ritually unclean. You are, in fact, pregnant right now, carrying a son. No razor will touch his head—the boy will be God's Nazirite from the moment of his birth. He will launch the deliverance from Philistine oppression (Judges 13:3-5).

During the forty years spent wandering in the wilderness, God had given Moses a series of laws and rituals for the people to follow. The majority of the Books of Leviticus and Numbers provide the details of all God's laws and rituals. The main emphasis of all the rules and regulations God gave Moses was on helping the Children of Israel live in a proper relationship with Almighty God.

One special option for any Israelite man or woman was to take a Nazirite vow—

> Speak to the People of Israel; tell them, If any of you, man or woman, wants to make a special Nazirite vow, consecrating yourself totally to God, you must not drink any wine or beer, no intoxicating drink of any kind, not even the juice of grapes—in fact, you must not even eat grapes or raisins. For the duration of the consecration, nothing from the grapevine—not even the seeds, not even the skin—may be eaten. Also, for the duration of the consecration you must not have your hair cut. Your long hair will be a continuing sign of holy separation to God. Also, for the duration of the consecration to God, you must not go near a corpse. Even if it's the body of your father or mother, brother or sister, you must not ritually defile yourself because the sign of consecration to God is on your head. For the entire duration of your consecration you are holy to God (Numbers 6:1-8).

Three things marked the individual making a special Nazirite vow—

- Total and complete abstinence from alcoholic beverages and grapes.
- Total and complete abstinence from death and dead bodies—animal and human.
- Total and complete abstinence from cutting one's hair.

Throughout his life, Samson was set apart by God to live in a holy relationship with Him. Samson was to never drink wine—or even taste grapes, raisins, or grape juice. Samson was to never be near or touch a dead body—human or animal. And Samson was to never have his hair cut—ever.

Unfortunately, on each and every count, Samson selfishly and sinfully violated his vow.

- He went out of his way to see what was left of a dead lion... (see Judges 14:5-9)
- He had a feast (including wine consumption) at his wedding... (see Judges 14:10-20)
- And, he had his hair cut by Delilah... (see Judges 16:4-20)

In spite of his abject failure at keeping his Nazirite vow, and in spite of his willful sins, God still used Samson as judge in Israel for twenty years.

Born under the promise of God's presence and strength, Samson had some of the greatest potential of any human ever conceived. With the hand of God on him, Samson could have followed God and led Israel to heights unseen. Unfortunately, his capacity for selfishness doomed him. Samson's disobedience almost certainly delayed Israel's release from the Philistine oppression.

Samson was especially self-centered and sinful when it came to the women in his life. First, he wanted a Philistine wife because "she's the one I want" (Judges 14:3). Later, he slept with a prostitute (see Judges 16:1-3). And, in the story we all know, Samson allowed his lust for Delilah to blind him to her traps (see Judges 14:4-20).

In spite of all his selfishly sinful shortcomings, sexual and otherwise, Samson is still used by God to free the Hebrews nation from the Philistines.

After being shaved bald, taken captive, and having his eyes plucked out, the Philistines treated Samson like a circus freak show. Whenever there was a party, or opportunity, Philistine royalty and society trotted out Samson for an evening of ridicule and spectacle.

Ultimately, in his last act, Samson lived and died in "God's Strength."

They got Samson from the prison and he put on a show for them. They had him standing between the pillars. Samson said to the young man who was acting as his guide, 'Put me where I can touch the pillars that hold up the temple so I can rest against them.' The building was packed with men and women, including all the Philistine tyrants. And there were at least three thousand in the stands watching Samson's performance. And Samson cried out to God: 'Master, God! Oh, please, look on me again, Oh, please, give strength yet once more. God! With one avenging blow let me be avenged on the Philistines for my two eyes!' Then Samson reached out to the two central pillars that held up the building and pushed against them, one with his right arm, the other with his left. Saying, 'Let me die with the Philistines,' Samson pushed hard with all his might. The building crashed on the tyrants and all the people in it. He killed more people in his death than he had killed in his life (Judges 16:25-30).

Some might say God's imposing the Nazirite standard on Samson made his life impossible from his conception. Some might say Samson was doomed to failure without any choice in the matter. And whenever Samson relied on his own strength or his own capacity for riddle-making, he was doomed. He did fail. Yet, as the last act of his life showed, whenever Samson called out to and relied on "God's Strength," he accomplished great things for God and God's kingdom.

Whenever we look at Samson, we are drawn to his strength. We love the superhero images of Samson with rippling muscles and long, flowing, golden locks of hair. We wish we could gaze in the mirror and see the strength and handsome good looks of Samson looking back at us.

Unfortunately, when we look for Samson in the mirror, what we see looking back at us is Samson's sin and disgrace. We see sin and disgrace that match our own sinfulness. In the mirror, we see God's Image reduced by the cracks and crevices of our own image.

Countless studies have been done to determine how we view God. In the vast majority of these quizzes, questionnaires, and tests, we design a Jesus who looks remarkably like our own self in personality and temperament.

Scot McKnight, professor of religious studies at North Park College in Chicago, says of such tests he has given over many years to his college students—"The test results also suggest that, even though we like to think we are becoming more like Jesus, the reverse is probably more the case: *we try to make Jesus like ourselves.*"[1]

In other words, we re-create God into our own images, making Him remarkably similar to our own self, all so we can sleep at night. After all, if God is like us, we must be doing okay.

The old saw says—"God created us in His Image... and we have been repaying the favor ever since." In some ways, this is to be expected as you and I take advantage of "God's Vulnerabilities" and "God's Position." Our "survival-of-the-fittest" mentality squashes out weakness. Because who wants a God with weaknesses, or vulnerabilities?

As we consider our relationship with God, we struggle with one issue above most others. No matter how hard we try to delude ourselves, we can't escape this question—

- How do I measure up?

The inescapable reality is this—

- God is holy, perfect, and just. No matter how hard I try, I am not. How do I measure up to Him?

On one hand, the devil is great at getting us to throw in the towel and say—"I don't—and can never—measure up to God..." This kind of fatalism can lead us to make rash decisions like Adam and Eve in the Garden of Eden.

On the other hand, we like to delude ourselves into believing we have evolved to become more sophisticated and refined than Adam and Eve. We refuse to just give up because the devil wants us to. In the delusion of our sophistication, we have designed a system of measurement by comparison. We like to look at others and say—"I am pretty good compared to..."

This method works especially well for us because we always pick people clearly worse than we are for the comparison—

- "I am pretty good compared to... Hitler, Stalin, or Pol Pot."
- "I am pretty good compared to... Bernie Madoff."
- "I am pretty good compared to... that drunk with the 'Will werk 4 food' sign sitting in the intersection by the grocery store."

Coupled with our creation of a God and Savior who is remarkably like us in temperament and character, we always come off looking pretty good.

Here, however, is The Truth—

- God measures everything by one measuring stick.
- God measures everything by Jesus.

Instead of being measured in comparison to others, God looks at us and sees His only-begotten Son, Jesus Christ. Instead of our sin, God sees Jesus. Instead of your arrogance and law-breaking sinfulness, "The Hero of Faithfulness" sees only His Son, Jesus Christ. God looks and His sight is filled with men and women in white robes. God's vision is like John's in Revelation 7—

> 'These in white robes—who are they, and where did they come from?' [John] answered, 'Sir, you know.' And [the angel of the Lord] said, 'These are they who have come out of the great tribulation; they have washed their robes and made them white in the blood of the Lamb' (Revelation 7:13-14, NIV).

"The Hero of Faithfulness" looks at us and sees Jesus Christ—"But if we walk in the light, as He is in the light, we have fellowship with one another, and the blood of Jesus, His Son, purifies us from all sin" (1 John 1:7, NIV).

Instead of being measured in comparison to God and His own Perfection, we are measured against the blood and righteousness of Jesus Christ, who purifies us and gives us new robes for life and eternal life.

In light of Samson's train-wreck of a life, we could try to measure ourselves against the muscle-bound shadow he cast.

However, the true tale of Samson's life is to remind us that everything we do is done because of "God's Strength" in us.

Because of "God's Strength" we can assume the standard by which Paul chose to live—

I eagerly expect and hope that I will in no way be ashamed, but will have sufficient courage so that now as always Christ will be exalted in my body, whether by life or by death. For to me, to live is Christ and to die is gain. If I am to go on living in the body, this will mean fruitful labor for me. Yet what shall I choose? I do not know! I am torn between the two: I desire to depart and be with Christ, which is better by far; but it is more necessary for you that I remain in the body (Philippians 1:20-24, NIV).

At the end of his life, Samson was made a spectacle of one last time. Yet from behind blind eyes, Samson must have finally been able to clearly see the Light of God's leading.

As he was pushing on those columns, trying to bring down the house in his encore performance, delivering Israel from the Philistine oppressors, Samson must have seen the reality of living "God's Strength"—"Alive, I'm Christ's messenger; dead, I'm His bounty. Life versus even more life! I can't lose" (Philippians 1:21).

In "God's Strength," neither can you!

Chapter 19

"Jephthah: God's Promise"

My first pastorate was at Mammoth Lakes Lutheran Church, in Mammoth Lakes, California. For the last several years I was pastor in Mammoth, I would join a couple other local pastors on a weekly radio program. "The Pastors' Round Table" was a half-hour program aired every Sunday morning on KDAY-FM.

Somehow or other, Thin Lizzy's classic rock song "The Boys Are Back In Town" became our theme song. Each week, we would cue up the sound of motorcycles revving their engines and Thin Lizzy would belt out—

> Guess who just got back today?
> Them wild-eyed boys that had been away
> Haven't changed, haven't much to say
> But man, I still think them cats are crazy
> They were asking if you were around
> How you was, where you could be found
> Told them you were living downtown
> Driving all the old men crazy
> The boys are back in town. . .[1]

I'll wait while you take a few minutes searching out a YouTube rendition of this classic. . .

Ready to continue?

"Jephthah: God's Promise"

Unlike the storyline in "The Boys Are Back In Town," none of us were motorcycle riders. And, unless the conversation turned to the Rapture, the End Times, or Baptism practices, none of us would have been considered "wild-eyed."

As we move along in the litany of men listed in verse 32, however, we are turning to a man who could legitimately play "The Boys Are Back In Town" as his theme song. Jephthah is the real deal when it comes to biblical characters who could double as biker dudes.

When I conjure up images of Jephthah, I picture a guy standing about 6'5", crunching a solid 12-pack of abs, with 24" pythons for biceps. In my vision, Jephthah weighs a solid 300 pounds. Under his leather jacket, he's got full-sleeve tats on both arms. Beyond his ears, he probably has some additional piercings we don't want to know anything about. His hair is tied in a slightly graying ponytail and he is sporting a thick, full, Fu Manchu moustache.

As Jephthah rides onto Scripture's stage, my vision places him astride the biggest, baddest Harley-Davidson motorcycle to ever roll out of Milwaukee. Behind him is a long line of fellow riders sporting an impressive array of bikes, leather, tats, piercings, and chains.

These images from the fertile soil of my imagination raise a question—

- How does a guy described as "one tough warrior" and the leader of "riffraff" (Judges 11:1-3) ever get to be a judge over Israel?
- Assuming the answer to this question can be figured out... why does this same rebel get mentioned in the litany of saints in Hebrews 11?

Continuing the theory that Hebrews 11:32 lists three pairs of characters, Jephthah is the tag-team partner of Samson.

For those of you with childhood memories watching professional wrestling—Bruiser Brody, Dusty Rhodes, the Junkyard Dog, anyone?—on a small black and white TV in the late 1970s and early 1980s, picture great tag-team partners like "The Road Warriors"— Hawk and Animal. Or perhaps, "The Fabulous Freebirds"—Michael Hayes and Terry "Bam-Bam" Gordy.

Samson would be the wrestling partner whose arsenal of moves was based on pure strength. Samson is the tag-team partner whose strength got him double-teamed and in trouble inside the squared-circle.

Jephthah would be the tag-team partner with the big mouth. His microphone skills and trash talking ways would always put their championship belts at risk. Yet, somehow, through a series of high-flying, high-risk maneuvers (and maybe a pair of brass knucks pulled out of his wrestling tights!), Jephthah would end up pinning the opponent and winning the match. As the referee raised their hands in victory, the arena sound system would reverberate with the motorcycle sounds of "The Boys Are Back In Town."

No two ways about it, Samson and Jephthah make one intimidating pair. But of all the men and women in Scripture, why are Samson and Jephthah included as a tag-team in Hebrews 11?

The story of Jephthah, the warrior from Gilead, is recorded in Judges 11 and 12. The heart of his life can be summarized like this—

- Jephthah was the illegitimate son of a man in Gilead. . .
- The "legitimate" sons threw him out of the family. . .
- Abandoned, Jephthah formed a gang of toughs and riff-raff living in the rugged part of the land. . .
- Meanwhile, the Ammonites oppressed Gilead and all of Israel. . .
- When the going got tough, Jephthah's brothers decided their illegitimate, gang-leader brother might not be so bad. . .
- Jephthah forged an agreement that would make him leader of the people if he got rid of the Ammonites. . .

In a scene straight from the smoke-filled backrooms inhabited by professional wrestling's match-makers and script-writers—"Then Jephthah sent messengers to the king of the Ammonites with a message: 'What's going on here that you have come into my country picking a fight?'" (Judges 11:12).

The ensuing smack-talk between Jephthah and the king of the Ammonites quickly escalated because "the king of the Ammonites refused to listen to a word that Jephthah had sent him" (Judges 11:28).

It took no time at all for the raw emotions to set a stage for one final smackdown.

Before going into battle, Jephthah can't help himself. He pops off at the mouth one more time—

> Jephthah made a vow before God: 'If You give me a clear victory over the Ammonites, then I'll give to God whatever comes out of the door of my house to meet me when I return in one piece from among the Ammonites—I'll offer it up in a sacrificial burnt offering' (Judges 11:30-31).

The battle that followed was as one-sided as any recorded in Scripture. Jephthah's band of thugs crushed the Ammonites. From one end of the country to the other—and everywhere in between—Jephthah and his rebels massacred the Ammonites.

With the high emotions of a sweet victory propelling him home, Jephthah's "daughter ran from the house to welcome him home—dancing to tambourines! She was his only child. He had no son or daughter except her" (Judges 11:34).

As the words of his own rash vow came screaming back at him—"I'll offer it up in a sacrificial burnt offering"—Jephthah's heart caught in his throat. "When he realized who it was, [Jephthah] ripped his clothes, saying, 'Ah, dearest daughter—I'm dirt. I'm despicable. My heart is torn to shreds. I made a vow to God and I can't take it back!'" (Judges 11:35).

In some of the most difficult, heart-rending words found anywhere in the Bible, Jephthah's daughter says—

> Dear father, if you made a vow to God, do to me what you vowed; God did His part and saved you from your Ammonite enemies... But let this one thing be done for me. Give me two months to wander through the hills and lament my virginity since I will never marry, I and my dear friends (Judges 11:36-37).

At this point, there is division among theologians over whether or not Jephthah followed through and kept his rash vow or not.

Some scholars would like to see a symbolic interpretation in the daughter's "roaming the hills." They hold that Jephthah tempered his vow by banishing his daughter to a life of exile with no hope of rejoining society. Supposedly, Jephthah made his daughter live out her days as a virgin—alone, with no hope of a husband, children, or a family.

Other scholars hold that after her two months of preparation and lament, Jephthah followed through, kept his vow, and sacrificed his daughter's life.

The Scriptures say—"He sent her off for two months. She and her dear girlfriends went among the hills, lamenting that she would never marry. At the end of the two months, she came back to her father. He fulfilled the vow with her that he had made. She had never slept with a man" (Judges 11:38-39).

As troubling as the question of whether or not Jephthah really did sacrifice his daughter's life is, the larger question is—

- If Hebrews 11 really has partnered Jephthah and Samson, what do they teach us about "The Hero of Faithfulness" and His attributes?

Samson's parents, childless until God's angel favored them with their son, raised him in a nurturing home. Samson was dedicated to live the vow of a Nazirite. But Samson recklessly, selfishly, and repeatedly broke every part of the Nazirite vow.

Samson's life could be summarized—

- "Holy Vow... Broken Vow..."

Jephthah, on the other hand, was the son of a whore. He was the throw-away child of his father's illicit dalliance. He had nothing and what little he did have was taken from him. Jephthah lived the careless, selfish life of a rebel, including making one too many rash vows that came back to haunt him.

Certainly, everyone would have understood if Jephthah had broken his word. Most people probably expected Jephthah to go back on his vow. It would have been understandable if he offered up a couple bulls or a flock of goats as an alternate sacrifice. But "he fulfilled the vow with her that he had made" (Judges 11:39).

Jephthah's life could be summarized—

- "Rash Vow. . . Kept Vow. . ."

In many ways, the lives of Samson and Jephthah parallel Jesus' "Parable of the Two Sons"—

A man had two sons. He went up to the first and said, 'Son, go out for the day and work in the vineyard.' The son answered, 'I don't want to.' Later on he thought better of it and went. The father gave the same command to the second son. He answered, 'Sure, glad to.' But he never went (Matthew 21:28-30).

The second son in the parable, like Samson, said he would go and work for his father, but he didn't. Good start. Bad finish.

The first son in Jesus' story, paralleling Jephthah, ignored his father's request, but, in the end, he does go and work for his father. Bad start. Good finish.

Jesus' question about which son did what his father wanted brings the making and keeping of vows to the center of the reason why both Samson and Jephthah are included in Hebrews 11. The heart of the matter is whether or not words have meaning—our words and, more importantly, God's words.

James 5 tells us—"Above all, my brothers, do not swear—not by heaven or by earth or by anything else. Let your 'Yes' be yes, and your 'No,' no, or you will be condemned" (James 5:12, NIV).

Because words—and oaths and vows—do have meaning, we are to be extremely careful with what we say.

- Don't speak before thinking.
- Don't embellish.
- Don't let your words be your trap.

Our words do have meaning. But even more so do God's words have meaning! Never forget! Always remember! "The Hero of Faithfulness" is a God of WORDS!

By His WORDS, God created everything out of nothing.

By WORDS spoken to Adam and Eve, God promised the world a Messiah.

Through WORDS, God called Abram to be the Father of His People.

Using WORDS, God spoke to His People through judges, like Samson and Jephthah.

In keeping His WORD, the God of WORDS became flesh and was born of a virgin.

In Jesus Christ, the WORD dwelt for 33 years among us full of grace and truth.

Ultimately, the WORD became flesh kept His WORD—"When He had received the drink, Jesus said, 'It is finished.' With that, He bowed His head and gave up His spirit" (John 19:30, NIV).

As Paul puts it to the Corinthians—

No matter how many promises God has made, they are 'Yes' in Christ. And so through Him the 'Amen' is spoken by us to the glory of God. Now it is God who makes both us and you stand firm in Christ. He anointed us, set His seal of ownership on us, and put His Spirit in our hearts as a deposit, guaranteeing what is to come (2 Corinthians 1:20-22, NIV).

God is "destined to complete" what He started.
God is bound to keep His WORD of guarantee.

Against the backdrop of Samson—"Holy Vow. . . Broken Vow"— and Jephthah—"Rash Vow. . . Kept Vow"—what did Jesus come for?

Jesus—the WORD of God—left heaven to live among us.
Jesus—the WORD of God—endured pain and punishment beyond belief for us.
Jesus—the WORD of God—died a brutal death on a cross for us.
Jesus—the WORD of God—rose from death in victory for us.

Jesus—the WORD of God—ascended into heaven, but is still always with us.

Jesus—the WORD of God—kept "God's Promise" for us.

Here is something to ponder as this chapter draws to a close—

- Did Jesus—the WORD of God manifest in human flesh—do all this so we could give Him half-hearted, lip-service worship?
- Are our broken vows and forgotten faith what heaven rejoices over?

Hardly!

Because of the WORD of God keeping His WORD in Jesus Christ, we have been forgiven, saved, blessed, gifted, and sent!

Ultimately, together with Samson, Jephthah reminds us that "God's Promise"—by the power of His WORD—redeems us and makes us His own.

Chapter 20

"David: God's Heart"

*I*f the earlier chapter on Samson began with a brain-stimulating exercise, then let's get this chapter started by getting the blood flowing...

Up on your feet—

- Stand with your feet shoulder width apart...
- With your hands on your hips, bend over at the waist...
- Stare into your own belly button...

While holding this pose and continuing your staredown with your belly button, ask yourself this question—

- As I am gazing at my navel—what can I really see?

Newsflash—navel-gazing severely limits your ability to see anything but your own stomach.

St. Paul knew what he was talking about when he told the Philippians—

> For, as I have often told you before and now say again even with tears, many live as enemies of the cross of Christ. Their destiny is destruction, their god is their stomach, and their glory is in their shame. Their mind is on earthly things (Philippians 3:18-19, NIV)

The Christian Church in the United States of America has been doing a lot of navel-gazing in recent decades. We don't do it intentionally. We don't "glory in our shame" on purpose. We don't make a god out of our stomachs on purpose.

However, have you ever heard anyone say something along the lines of—

- "Prosperity can be a more difficult trial than poverty."

Considering the prosperous (READ: American Christians) know their next meal is assured, while about one billion people on the planet don't know if there will even be a next meal...

Considering the prosperous (READ: Christians in the United States of America) are the most affluent people in the history of the world, while almost three billion people on our big, blue marble scratch and claw to eke out an existence on less than $2 a day...

Considering the prosperous (READ: YOU & ME!) have more religious rights, liberties, and freedoms than anyone ever before in human history, while followers of Jesus Christ around the world are being persecuted and killed EVERY DAY...

To hold any facet of thought that prosperity can be a more difficult trial than poverty is a grotesquely American Christian way of assuaging the guilt of our hedonistic affluenza.

This is a strong statement.

But fat and sassy American Christians—when our minds are influenced, as Saint Paul says, by "earthly things," it is an accurate declaration.

Continuing into the six-pack of men listed in Hebrews 11:32, the final pair of characters speaks directly to the troubles that result from navel-gazing, self-centeredness, and the influence of "earthly things."

David and Samuel, two of the greatest leaders Israel ever knew, help us see "God's Heart" and "God's Ear" at work in our affluent lives.

Just as a refresher, listen again to Hebrews 11:32—"I could go on and on, but I've run out of time. There are so many more—Gideon, Barak, Samson, Jephthah, David, Samuel, the prophets" (Hebrews 11:32).

David—the greatest king Israel ever knew.

King David—led the nation of Israel to its greatest military and political heights.

King David—wrote over half the psalms.

King David—about whom more of the Old Testament speaks than anyone else.

King David—the ultimate Renaissance man, 2500 years before the Renaissance!

David—is listed in Hebrews 11 with no description!

Enoch got two verses. 12 verses—Hebrews 11:8-19—deal with Abraham, Sarah, and Isaac. Even "the harlot Rahab" got a whole verse to herself.

It almost seems like the author of Hebrews thinks to include David as an afterthought.

Can you picture the author looking over what he had written. Checking the list. Nodding at Abel. Smiling at Moses and the Red Sea. Starting to roll up his scroll. Stopping suddenly. Smacking his forehead with his palm. Quickly grabbing his quill and ink, while exclaiming, "Oh yeah! I better include David!"

How can David be lumped in with five other guys and be given absolutely no description?

In 1 Samuel 13, Samuel tells Saul, Israel's first king, that God no longer favors him. Samuel says—

> "You acted foolishly. . . You have not kept the command the Lord your God gave you; if you had, He would have established your kingdom over Israel for all time. But now your kingdom will not endure; the Lord has sought out a man after His own heart and appointed him leader of His people, because you have not kept the Lord's command (1Samuel 13:13-14, NIV).

Regardless of how much or how little is said about David in Hebrews 11, the crux of why he is included is found in Samuel's first unnamed reference to him. From before he was ever introduced onto Scripture's stage, David already was receiving the highest accolades ever given to any human—he was a man seeking after God's own heart.

When David enters the biblical record a few chapters later in 1 Samuel, it is almost humorous. After rejecting Saul, God sends Samuel to the hill country around Bethlehem on a quest to anoint the next king. At the home of Jesse, Samuel announces he is there to teach a worship seminar. As part of the preparation, Jesse's eldest son, Eliab, struts past Samuel. Impressed by Eliab's build and looks, Samuel thinks he has found the next king. But—NO!

God says—"Looks aren't everything. Don't be impressed with his looks and stature. I've already eliminated him. God judges persons differently than humans do. Men and women look at the face; God *looks into the heart*" (1 Samuel 16:7, italics added).

Again, with a heart reference.

This same scene of divine rejection is repeated as all seven sons of Jesse present themselves to Samuel. With a hint of frustration in his voice, Samuel says—

> "Is this it? Are there no more sons?" "Well, yes, there's the runt. But he's out tending the sheep." So Samuel orders Jesse—"Go get him. We're not moving from this spot until he's here." (1 Samuel 16:11)

Jesse's "Oh-Yeah-I-Barely-Remembered-Fathering-An-8th-Son" is brought from watching the sheep out in the fields to walk before Samuel.

As soon as "the runt" gets close, God says—

> 'Up on your feet! Anoint him! This is the one.' Samuel took his flask of oil and anointed him, with his brothers standing around watching. The Spirit of God entered David like a rush of wind, God vitally empowering him for the rest of his life (1 Samuel 16:12b-13).

When Saul was chosen by God, he was the first "Made-for-TV" king. Saul was tall, dark, and handsome. He was photogenic and telegenic. Saul was everything Washington, D.C., looks for in a 21st century presidential candidate. And it was only 1000BC!

Given how Saul's reign was turning out, when He sought a second king, God went to the other end of the spectrum. Instead of the man head and shoulders above everyone else, God chose "the runt." But God knew "the runt" was going to be a man after His own heart.

Immediately following his secret anointing in Bethlehem, David enters Saul's service as a royal musician. David's exceptional musical skills soothed the black moods of depression Saul endured after the Holy Spirit left him.

Stop and think about this.

David's first stop on the path to becoming Israel's greatest king is to serve the current, out-of-divine-favor king. Talk about a role requiring humility. Even if David did not fully understand what Samuel had done to him back there in Bethlehem, he had to have recognized there was going to be a problem with King Saul someday. Yet David still did everything he could to soothe Saul's soul.

Soon after becoming Saul's musician, the Israelite army engaged in a stand-off with the Philistine army. For forty days, twice a day, the Philistine giant Goliath taunted the terrified Israelite army. Eighty times Goliath shouted across the valley—

> Why bother using your whole army? Am I not Philistine enough for you? And you're all committed to Saul, aren't you? So pick your best fighter and pit him against me. If he gets the upper hand and kills me, the Philistines will all become your slaves. But if I get the upper hand and kill him, you'll all become our slaves and serve us. I challenge the troops of Israel this day. Give me a man. Let us fight it out together! (1 Samuel 17:8-10).

Almost two months into this stand-off, Jesse sent his runt-son from Bethlehem with supplies for his oldest brothers who were in the stalemated Israelite army. When David arrived at the camp, he heard Goliath taunting the Israelites—and, worse, the God of Israel.

The story that unfolds is among the most well-known in the entire Bible. David slaying Goliath is a staple of Sunday School flannel boards from all times and in all places.

When you read 1 Samuel 17, verses 1-30 set the stage and verses 41-58 detail the battle and its aftermath. DO NOT hurry to the battle scene and skip the critical verses in the middle! David learns what might be his greatest lesson in pursuing "God's Heart" in verses 31-40.

The scene, in verse 31, opens as Saul gets wind of David's desire to fight Goliath. Saul thinks David is too small and inexperienced to fight such a massive and skilled foe as Goliath. But nowhere does Saul waste a nano-second thinking about taking on Goliath himself. After forty days of Goliath's taunts, Saul could probably recite the speech as Goliath delivered it.

In response to Saul's doubts, David isn't swayed or slowed—

I've been a shepherd, tending sheep for my father. Whenever a lion or bear came and took a lamb from the flock, I'd go after it, knock it down, and rescue the lamb. If it turned on me, I'd grab it by the throat, wring its neck, and kill it. Lion or bear, it made no difference—I killed it. And I'll do the same to this Philistine pig who is taunting the troops of God-Alive. God, who delivered me from the teeth of the lion and the claws of the bear, will deliver me from this Philistine (1Samuel 17:34-37).

Don't you love it!
"I've killed bear and lion. Killing a pig is no problem!"
Why not?
God will deliver me!

Here comes one of the most important parts of the entire episode. Saul agrees to let David fight for Israel. Saul even "outfitted David as a soldier in armor. He put his bronze helmet on his head and belted his sword on him over the armor. David tried to walk but he could hardly budge" (1 Samuel 17:38). Saul outfits David for battle, but Saul's armor didn't fit David. David couldn't move, let alone fight in Saul's armor.

So David took it all off. No helmet. No sword. No belt. No armor at all. David was used to fighting barehanded with whatever sticks and stones were nearby.

Lest you forget—David is going to face Goliath. Nearly ten feet tall. Wearing over 125 pounds of armor. Carrying a spear like a railroad tie. The tip of Goliath's spear alone weighed over fifteen pounds!

Instead of the finest armor in the Israelite army, David grabbed his shepherd staff and, down by the creek side, he selected five smooth stones, which he put in his leather pouch.

THE Hero of Faithfulness

The match-up at the Alamo was more even! David Crockett stood a better chance against Santa Ana and the Mexican Army!

David versus Goliath is a bigger mismatch than the proverbial bringing of a knife to a gunfight. David's battle against Goliath is more like a child with a plastic butter knife fighting against an Uzi-wielding Rambo wearing several bandoliers of extra ammunition.

Sticks and stones against the greatest fighting machine known to civilization.

Is David out of his mind turning down Saul's armor? Who cares if it doesn't fit quite right? What Saul offered David had just come from the Israelite War Department's Research and Development division. Saul's armor was the finest, most technologically advanced in the possession of the Israelites.

David was being. . . what?

Foolish? Crazy? Impulsive?

How could he not want to secure all the protection possible for this battle?

Then again, maybe David already had secured all the protection possible, necessary, and available, when he said—"God will deliver me from this Philistine."

David's first and greatest lesson in pursuing "God's Heart" was realizing who he was and how God had made him.

David was not Saul. David had never fought a battle in full armor.

David was a shepherd. David did battle with sticks, stones, and bare hands.

David trusted that God had prepared him for this fight against Goliath by having him cross paths with all those lions and bears.

David relied on God's training.

David stepped out to fight Goliath as himself.

Of course, we know how the battle turned out. David faced off against Goliath with his slingshot and five smooth stones. Goliath laughed. David charged straight toward the giant. One stone whistled through the air until it landed with a "THWACK!" in the middle of Goliath's forehead. And the ground shook as the giant was felled by an eternal headache.

Pursuing "God's Heart" begins when we recognize the uniquenesses God has created into each of us. None of us are the same. Every single person is a unique character God has created.

"God's Heart" is forever interested in the unique and special relationship He can have with every one of His creations.

- God doesn't want to love you the same way He loves me.
- Neither does He want to love me like He loves you.

Our God is not a "One-Size-Fits-All" (or, as clothes now say—"One-Size-Fits-Most"!) God.

"God's Heart" is filled with special and specific love for each and every unique and creative need every single one of us have.

"God's Heart" uniquely and specifically pours His love into you as is required ONLY BY YOU!

Blaise Pascal, 17th century French mathematician and philosopher, said—"There is a God shaped vacuum in the heart of every man which cannot be filled by any created thing, but only by God, the Creator, made known through Jesus"[1]

This "God shaped vacuum" is specifically sized in each of us. This "God shaped hole" is different in every one of us.

- Your hole can't be filled with the love God wants to give me.
- Neither can my vacuum be filled with the love God has prepared for you.

The first lesson in becoming persons (plural, collective, all of us) who pursue the heart of God is to be the person (individual, singular, YOU) whom God created you to be!

David learned this lesson. As soon as he picked up and tried on Saul's armor, he knew what was wrong. Instead of doing what seemed intellectually rational, with foolish spiritual abandon, David trusted God. With his eyes firmly fixed on God, David faced the giant with his measly collection of sticks and stones. With his eyes and mind lifted off of "earthly things," David succeeded in defeating the Philistine giant.

Here is the major question—

- Do you trust "God's Heart" enough to face your giants armed with the love and grace "The Hero of Faithfulness" has prepared specifically and purposefully for you?

If your answer is a trusting "Yes," then whatever your level of prosperity or poverty, you will be used by God to fell the giants of injustice and inequity that surround you.

When we allow God's Holy Spirit to fill our hearts with the specific, personal love God has for us, we will personify this truth—

There's far more to life for us. We're citizens of high heaven! We're waiting the arrival of the Savior, the Master, Jesus Christ, who will transform our earthy bodies into glorious bodies like His own. He'll make us beautiful and whole with the same powerful skill by which He is putting everything as it should be, under and around Him (Philippians 3:20-21).

Chapter 21

"Samuel: God's Ear"

*M*y last two years in college, I had the same roommate. Over the course of those two years, the same thing happened in our dorm room almost every night. Sometime between 11:00pm and 2:00am, whoever of us was last to go to bed would turn off the lights. But neither of us would turn off the stereo. Almost every night, we went to sleep with the stereo playing. I have no idea what our reasoning was. Probably laziness turned into a habit.

Almost twenty-five years later, I have recently "re-adopted" this old habit. Lately, I have been going to sleep with music in the background. More nights than not over the last several months, I have left the TV turned on to DISH Channel 930—"Piano and Guitar."

Hardly the classic rock pumping in my dorm room (of course, it wasn't "classic" then. . . it was current rock hits). . .

Even as I write the first draft of this chapter at my "office" in the Hailey Public Library, I have headphones on providing background music from Pandora Radio to my ears.

- What is it about needing noise that gives us some sense of security?
- Why does it seem we are almost afraid of silence?

We are following our look at "God's Heart" by looking now at "God's Ear." As we do, it is by divine alignment that the name Samuel in Hebrew is—"Shema-El." Two words that mean—"Hear God," or "God Hears."

Samuel is the perfect partner for David. If David portrayed the essence of "God's Heart," then the man named "Hear God" is the only individual to logically study next. After all, there is no heart without an ear at its center. Look and see what I mean—hEARt.

David reveals "God's Heart" and Samuel shows us how "God's Ear" is at the center of His hEARt.

In Deuteronomy 6:4, "The Great Shema," the "Great Hear," of the Hebrew faith, this declaration is made—"Hear, O Israel: The Lord our God, the Lord is One" (Deuteronomy 6:4, NIV).

The implications for living out this hearing follows in verse 5—"Love the Lord your God with all your heart and with all your soul and with all your strength" (Deuteronomy 6:5, NIV).

In what may be the least insightful statement made in this entire book—ears are for hearing!

Take your time picking yourself up off the floor!

Wait for your pulse to slow to normal!

Okay. . . now that you have recovered and are able to continue. . .

If the ears hanging on the sides of our heads really are for hearing, the great question becomes—

- What do you hear?

Put spiritually and personally—

- WHO do you hear?

The voices competing to be heard are all around us. The noise in our world is all-pervasive. Whether it is the "natural" sounds of traffic and human congestion, or the manufactured noise from television, radio, iPod, or MP3 player, our ears are under continual assault. With so much sound and so many noises always bombarding us, what will rise to the foreground to actually be that which you hear. . . and listen to. . . and respond to?

Against this noisy backdrop, we come to Samuel. Quite the opposite of 8th-born David, Samuel was the firstborn of his mother. With overwhelming gratitude at his conception and birth, Hannah dedicated Samuel to a life of service in the Temple.

After several years had passed, when the boy Samuel was serving in the Temple, Scripture tells us, the Lord audibly spoke to Samuel.

Hearing this voice, Samuel got up from his bed and went to see what old, blind Eli the priest needed. The old man probably called to Samuel frequently in the dark of night for a glass of warm milk, or some such need.

Three times this same scene repeated itself. Each time, Samuel got out of his bed and ran to Eli, saying—"Here I am." But Eli had never called him. Each time, God was calling Samuel.

Finally, "Eli told Samuel, 'Go and lie down, and if He calls you, say, "Speak, Lord, for Your servant is listening."' So Samuel went and lay down in his place" (1 Samuel 3:9b, NIV).

A fourth time, God called to Samuel. This time, Samuel stayed in his bed and he replied—"Speak, Lord, Your servant is listening."

Several issues could be raised about why it took Eli and Samuel so long to recognize the voice of God calling. As the period of the judges was drawing to a close, 1 Samuel 3:1 says—"The boy Samuel ministered before the Lord under Eli. In those days the word of the Lord was rare; there were not many visions" (1 Samuel 3:1, NIV). Given this fact, over his long life, Eli probably hadn't heard God's voice very often. Interesting implications there, considering Eli is the chosen priest of Israel.

Also, verse 7 says—"Now Samuel did not yet know the Lord: The word of the Lord had not yet been revealed to him" (1 Samuel 3:7, NIV). Sort of makes one wonder what kind of spiritual training Samuel had been receiving from Eli. He probably knew all there was to know about how to polish the temple candlesticks. Samuel could probably recite all the proper parts of ancient Israelite worship liturgies in grammatically perfect Hebrew. But had Samuel received proper (or, any?) spiritual training across his years at Eli's feet?

Regardless, Samuel responds to God's fourth call—"Speak, O Lord, Your servant is listening."

Then the Lord spoke to Samuel—"See, I am about to do something in Israel that will make the ears of everyone who hears of it tingle. . ." (1 Samuel 3:11, NIV).

From a period of silence covering many years, God chooses to speak to a boy named Samuel. God speaks to a child named "God Hears" and out of the darkness, Samuel "Hears God."

With all the noise and sound that pulsates through our eardrums, are we able to hear God?

If God were to call to you as He did to Samuel, what would your response be? Would you join Samuel saying—"Speak, O Lord, Your servant is listening"?

Or would you be more likely to say—"Listen, O Lord, Your servant is speaking!" Would you, then, immediately launch into a list of woes and wants without wondering why God was calling you?

I have a sinking suspicion we would be more prone to assault "God's Ear" with a never-ending litany of words and wishes and wants.

No doubt much of what we would lay before the Lord would be legitimate—

- Health for loved ones
- Provisions for the needy
- Justice for the oppressed

Inadequately, it seems much of our spiritual training has taught us that prayer is a verbal one-way street—we do all the talking. . . God does all the listening.

If prayer is communication with God, then He better get comfortable because I have a lot to tell Him!

"Listen, O Lord, Your servant is speaking. . ."

In the process of our telling God all we need Him to do on our behalf, we become susceptible to taking liberties with what God has already told us. Take "The Lord's Prayer" for example.

In Matthew 6, Jesus responds to His disciples' inquiry about how to pray, saying—

> This, then, is how you should pray: 'Our Father in heaven, hallowed be Your name, Your kingdom come, Your will be done on earth as it is in heaven. Give us today our daily bread. Forgive us our debts, as we also have forgiven our debtors. And

lead us not into temptation, but deliver us from the evil one' (Matthew 6:9-13, NIV).

Instead of prayers that follow the model Jesus gave us, our prayers have a tendency to reflect an adapted version of what Jesus taught—

- Our Father, who is in heaven, hallowed by Your name, rapture us to Your kingdom where Your will is done... get us out of earth and into happy heaven...[1]

Instead of listening to what God tells us about His Name, His Kingdom, and His Will, we tell God what we desire Him to do with His Name, Kingdom, and Will. As a result of our verbal assaults, God's Name is hallowed among us too irregularly. God's Kingdom is prayed for by us too infrequently. And, God's Will is done among us too inconsistently.

And we wonder why "God's Ear" doesn't seem to hear us very well...

If our prayer lives have become imbalanced by the overwhelming quantity of our sounds and speaking, then we might just need to begin a rebellion against the status quo. Instead of a pious, conforming prayer life, perhaps we need to renovate our prayer life into one of open rebellion.

If so, the first step toward a rebellious prayer life might just be to adopt Samuel's posture in 1 Samuel 3. Maybe we need to go to bed! Maybe we need to lay down, be still, and wait for God to speak.

Admittedly, we aren't good at waiting. And, we are pretty terrible at being patient.

Perhaps, the key to hearing God is to take the advice of Psalm 46:10 to hEARt and to put it into practice—"Be still, and know that I am God; I will be exalted among the nations, I will be exalted in the earth" (Psalm 46:10, NIV).

Samuel lays down and he is still. Then, from the still of the night, he hears God speaking.

Let's admit the truth. Our lives are far from still and we are almost never quiet. As a result, we are left wondering if God ever speaks.

Maybe our prayer lives really do need a bit of rebellion. Instead of maintaining the status quo, perhaps our first "prayer rebellion" against the status quo should be to practice stillness and listening.

The verbs in Psalm 46:10 don't leave any room for equivocation—

- "Be still. . . and know. . ."

Not—"Be still. . . and you might. . ."
Or—"Be still. . . and I could. . ."

- "Be still. . . and know. . . I AM God!"

In the movie *Forrest Gump*, the movie opens with Forrest Gump sitting on a park bench. As he begins telling his story (and if ever anyone could represent us talking too much, it would be Forrest Gump!), a single white feather floats into the scene. The (presumably) same feather appears at the end of the movie as Forrest Junior gets on the school bus.

Among many interpretations offered for what this feather symbolizes, is the role "dumb luck" plays in life. As Forrest's mother said—"Life is like a box of chocolates. You never know what you're going to get."

WRONG!

Prayer that proceeds from the hEARt of God to the lives of God's children is most certainly NOT like Forrest Gump's feather. There is absolutely no dumb luck or uncertain wind blowing God's personal desires for each of His Children to some random landing point.

Prayer that proceeds from the hEARt of God to the lives of God's children is certain to lead to God's will being done "on earth as it is in heaven."

Herein lies the greatest rebellion our prayer lives need. We need to hEAR God speak so we can live out what He says to us. Once we hEAR God, we will be able to act as Deuteronomy 6:5 says, with all our heart, soul, and strength serving God and those around us.

Several divine blessings result from this kind of rebellious prayer life.

First, when we hEAR God and put our hEARt, soul, and mind into His service, we will approach prayer like "The Parable of the Persistent Widow."

Luke 18:1 says—"Then [Jesus] spoke a parable to them, that men always ought to pray and not lose heart. . ." (Luke 18:1, NKJV).

The most important way to a rebellious prayer life is to pray "and not lose heart." Persistence is absolutely essential when we pray. We are to pray knowing "God's Ear" is always inclined toward us.

The widow in the parable Jesus told in Luke 18 badgered the judge continually because she was not willing to accept the status quo of her situation. Neither can we be resigned to accepting the status quo of our lives.

It may take a thousand sleepless nights for our prayers to receive God's answer. But persistence is the first facet of gaining "God's Ear."

After the judge gave in and helped the widow, Jesus explained His parable this way—

> Do you hear what that judge, corrupt as he is, is saying? So what makes you think God won't step in and work justice for His chosen people, who continue to cry out for help? Won't He stick up for them? I assure you, He will. He will not drag His feet. But how much of that kind of persistent faith will the Son of Man find on the earth when He returns? (Luke 18:6-8).

Rebellious prayer persistently refuses to accept the status quo.
Rebellious prayer persists against the pull to lose hEARt.

A second divine blessing that results from a rebellious prayer life is displayed in James 5. When we hEAR God and put our hEARt, soul, and mind into His service, we will approach prayer with the attitude James urges—

> Is anyone among you suffering? Let him pray. Is anyone cheerful? Let him sing psalms. Is anyone among you sick? Let him call for the elders of the church, and let them pray over him, anointing him with oil in the name of the Lord. And the prayer of faith will save the sick, and the Lord will raise

him up. And if he has committed sins, he will be forgiven (James 5:13-15, NKJV).

Prayer that rebels against the status quo is not the effort of a single, solitary soul.

Prayer that refuses to accept the status quo is to be a group effort.

Prayer that changes things calls on the entire family of faith to intercede for the sick and to celebrate for and with the healthy.

Prayer that rebels against the status quo also leads to new ways of living.

In *The Message*, James 5 continues—"Make this your common practice: Confess your sins to each other and pray for each other so that you can live together whole and healed" (James 5:16).

Confession of sins. Forgiveness and reconciliation between brothers and sisters. Wholeness and healing. These things are to be the "common practice" of a people living in open "prayer rebellion."

Rebellious prayer hEARs God—"Be still, and know that I am God. . ." (Psalm 46:10, NIV).

Rebellious prayer persists and does not lose hEARt. . .

Rebellious prayer commonly practices confession and healing. . .

Rebellious prayer begins—"Speak, O Lord, Your servant is listening. . ."

Rebellious prayer can probably turn off the noise generated by Dish channel 930 "Piano and Guitar" so we are able to sleep fitfully and peacefully through the night.

Chapter 22

"The Prophets: God's Focus"

*E*nvision a scene like this unfolding somewhere in heaven. . .

In a room reminiscent of a squad room on a police drama, angels amble in with their morning coffee in biodegradable, environmentally-friendly cups. The angels are bantering with one another as they take their seats on metal folding chairs. Archangels Gabriel and Michael assume their positions at the front of the room. Order comes quickly to the assembled legions.

From behind a pair of reading glasses, Gabriel studies some notes on the day's duty roster. Finally, he removes his glasses, looks up, and stares over the ranks of angels. At long last, he sighs and asks—"Who has anything to report?"

There is some nervous shifting of angelic behinds on the metal chairs. A few muffled coughs and muttered words are almost heard.

Timidly, one rookie angel raises his hand and speaks up—"Boss, nothing is happening. What are we supposed to report?"

Other angels quickly harmonize their agreement—

- "They don't do anything. . ."
- "They don't care. . ."
- "Nobody tries anything. . ."
- "Can I get a transfer. . ."
- "Does the choir have any openings. . ."

THE Hero of Faithfulness

With a flutter of his wings, Michael regains control of the briefing. Looking serious, he says—"I know these are lean times. I know it is difficult. You have important tasks to fulfill. You have to be ready at a moment's notice to move in and rescue them. Things won't—can't—remain this boring forever. Now get out there. Be safe. Keep them safe. Remember—you are guardian angels!"

As the rank and file guardian angels move out to begin their patrols, Gabriel looks at Michael—"Do you think today's Christians. . . especially the comfortable ones in the United States. . . will ever put their faith into action?"

Whether or not we really are boring our guardian angels to death, it is absolutely certain that no guardian angels were bored during the lives of those listed in Hebrews 11:32—"I could go on and on, but I've run out of time. There are so many more—Gideon, Barak, Samson, Jephthah, David, Samuel, the prophets. . ." (Hebrews 11:32).

Far from a boring afterthought to Hebrews 11, the men listed in verse 32 reveal some extremely important attributes of God's character. The tandem of Gideon and Barak display "God's Vulnerability" and "God's Position." The dynamic and muscle-bound duo of Samson and Jephthah give us insight into "God's Strength" and "God's Promise." The pair of David and Samuel help us discover "God's Heart" and "God's Ear."

Building on these partnerships, the author of Hebrews 11 climaxes his list with an entire category of people—"the prophets." Without names, he gives details about how "The Hero of Faithfulness" was focused on each prophet. Listen to the description Hebrews 11 gives to the period in which the prophets lived—

> Through acts of faith, they toppled kingdoms, made justice work, took the promises for themselves. They were protected from lions, fires, and sword thrusts, turned disadvantage to advantage, won battles, routed alien armies. Women received their loved ones back from the dead. There were those who, under torture, refused to give in and go free, preferring something better: resurrection. Others braved abuse and whips, and, yes, chains and dungeons. We have stories of those who were stoned, sawed in two, murdered in cold blood; stories of

vagrants wandering the earth in animal skins, homeless, friendless, powerless—the world didn't deserve them!—making their way as best they could on the cruel edges of the world (Hebrews 11:33-38).

Given the way some churches and denominations use titles—"Apostle Roberts," "Prophet Melissa"—to be called by God to be a prophet may sound exciting, or even romantic. But to be an Old Testament prophet came with the potential for some exceedingly extreme and bizarre actions.

Take the way God used Ezekiel as a visual aid. First, Ezekiel was bound hand and foot in his house for an unspecified period of time. He also had his tongue stuck to the roof of his mouth so he couldn't speak (see Ezekiel 3:24-27).

Later, Ezekiel got to lay on his left side without moving for 390 days. Then, he got to roll over and lay on his right side for another forty days. Over fourteen months laying in the dirt staring at a model he had made of Jerusalem under siege (see Ezekiel 4:1-8).

In preparation for the excitement of spending fourteen months laying around in the dirt, Ezekiel was to cook flatbread from a very specific recipe. He was also to bake his food over a fire stoked by human excrement. When Ezekiel complained about the poop-fire, God relented—slightly—and let him cook the bread over animal dung instead (see Ezekiel 4:9-13).

After those exciting fourteen months, Ezekiel got to shave his head and beard as yet another example of God's judgment (see Ezekiel 5:1-4).

At one point, Ezekiel was told by God his wife was going to die. However, when she did, he was not allowed to cry, weep, mourn, or show any signs of grief at her death (see Ezekiel 24:14-18).

Think Ezekiel had it hard? How about Hosea?

Hosea was told by God—"Find a whore and marry her. Make this whore the mother of your children. And here's why: This whole country has become a whorehouse, unfaithful to Me, God" (Hosea 1:2-3).

Because it is the way of my warped mind, I visualize the day God approached Hosea with his plan like this—

God: "Hosea, how are you doing?"

Hosea: "Hey, God. I'm okay. I was just thinking about that cute girl who lives across the street."

God: "Forget about her, Hosea. Have I got the girl for you! I want you to marry the hooker who works the corner of Clinton and 43rd Streets."

Hosea: "You want me to do what, God?"

God (suddenly sounding more like James Earl Jones than George Burns): "You heard Me. Marry a hooker."

Hosea: "Are you sure, God?"

God: "Yes. I AM sure. I have My reasons."

Hosea: "Okay. If You say so. But can I ask one question?"

God: "I suppose one question is okay."

Hosea: "I'll marry that hooker because You want me to. But. . . I mean. . . does she really have to be named Gomer?"

Three children later, Gomer abandoned her marriage to Hosea so she could return to prostitution. Instead of letting her go, God told Hosea to go find her, forgive her, take her back, and continue being husband to her (see Hosea 3).

Still think being called by God to be a prophet sounds romantic?

Isaiah also got to spend some quality time as a visual parable—"In the year the field commander, sent by King Sargon of Assyria, came to Ashdod and fought and took it, God told Isaiah son of Amoz, 'Go, take off your clothes and sandals,' and Isaiah did it, going about naked and barefooted" (Isaiah 20:1-2).

Not since Adam and Eve went looking for fig leaves in the Garden of Eden back in Genesis 3 has there been nudity like this in the Bible!

Oh. . . and keep reading in Isaiah 20—"Then God said, 'Just as My servant Isaiah has walked around town naked and barefooted for three years as a warning sign. . .'" (Isaiah 20:3).

3 years baring it all!

Isaiah walked around town for 3 years looking like "The Naked Cowboy" in Times Square—except "The Naked Cowboy" wears underwear! (Hold on to that underwear image for a moment...)

Hebrews 11:37 says some prophets were "sawed in two." According to tradition that was Isaiah's fate. As he tried to hide from history's most evil king of Israel, King Manasseh, Isaiah was captured and, according to legend, sawed into pieces for being a faithful prophet of God's Word.

Remember Isaiah's nudity and "The Naked Cowboy's" underwear? A couple hundred years after Isaiah's streak as "The Naked Prophet," God spoke to Jeremiah and told him to go "and buy yourself some linen shorts. Put them on and keep them on. Don't even take them off to wash them" (Jeremiah 13:1).

After wearing his tightie-whities for some (really smelly) period of time, God told Jeremiah to go on a lengthy trip to the region of the Euphrates River in Babylon, strip off his BVDs, and bury his boxers by the Euphrates River.

Then—

> ...after quite a long time, God told me, 'Go back to [the Euphrates] and get the linen shorts I told you to hide there.' So I went back to [the Euphrates] and dug them out of the place where I had hidden them. The shorts by then had rotted and were worthless. God explained, 'This is the way I am going to ruin the pride of Judah and the great pride of Jerusalem... They're going to turn out as rotten as these old shorts... (Jeremiah 13:6-11).

How's that for following God's call on your life?

Jeremiah was also beaten several times (presumably not because of the odor of his drawers!). Once after a beating, he was put in the stocks in the town square (see Jeremiah 20:1-2). Another time after being beaten, Jeremiah was imprisoned (see Jeremiah 37:14-16). Yet another time, Jeremiah was beaten and thrown into a cistern and left to wallow and die in the mud (see Jeremiah 38:6). No wonder Jeremiah is called "The Weeping Prophet"—he was always crying as he licked his wounds after getting beat up!

If Isaiah is the prophet in Hebrews 11:37 "sawed in two," tradition believes Jeremiah is the prophet who was "stoned to death."

Neither Isaiah's, nor Jeremiah's deaths are recorded in Scripture, so all we have to go on is historical speculation. The only Old Testament prophet to be explicitly killed and have his death recorded in the Bible is Zechariah, the son of Jehoiada the priest. For speaking God's Word, Zechariah managed to get on the wrong side of King Joash and the leadership of Judah—

> Then the Spirit of God moved Zechariah son of Jehoiada the priest to speak up: 'God's word: Why have you deliberately walked away from God's commandments? You can't live this way! If you walk out on God, He'll walk out on you.' But they worked out a plot against Zechariah, and with the complicity of the king—he actually gave the order!—they murdered him, pelting him with rocks, right in the court of The Temple of God. That's the thanks King Joash showed the loyal Jehoiada, the priest who had made him king. He murdered Jehoiada's son. Zechariah's last words were, 'Look, God! Make them pay for this!' (2 Chronicles 24:20-22).

Indeed, as Hebrews 11 says with decided understatement—"the world didn't deserve them" (Hebrews 11:38).

Just as "the world didn't deserve them," so also God did not desert them. "The Hero of Faithfulness" remained with every single prophet He called into service. As the great hymn "Amazing Grace" says, God was focused on seeing their faith "through many dangers, toils, and snares."

As you think about the bizarre and challenging actions God required of His prophets—

- What is God requiring of you?
- What is God asking you to do?

Perhaps more important, as you think about Ezekiel, Hosea, Isaiah, Jeremiah, Zechariah, and all the other prophets—

- Do you think God is asking too much of you?

"The Prophets: God's Focus"

The fact that you are reading this book is proof that you haven't been sawed in two, stoned, or killed for your faith.

God hasn't asked you to lay down your life for Him. . . yet!

And even if God does call for you to make that ultimate sacrifice? So what?

Even if God requires persecution or martyrdom of you, Paul gives us the greatest reminder of how to deal with life and death—"For to me, to live is Christ and to die is gain" (Philippians 1:21, NIV).

Along the way, Paul adds—"Whatever happens, conduct yourselves in a manner worthy of the gospel of Christ" (Philippians 1:27, NIV).

"God's Focus" on His prophets and all His children is three-fold—

- "God's Focus" is on filling us with His Holy Spirit and with power. . .
- "God's Focus" is on leading us where He desires. . .
- "God's Focus" is on protecting us through everything. . .

We love the first piece of this equation. We are great at asking God to fill us with the Holy Spirit. We crave being filled with God's power.

The second part of "God's Focus" gets a little trickier. We say we want to follow where God is leading. BUT. . .

That one word says it all—BUT. . .

"God's Focus" is on leading us where He desires. BUT. . . we want to dictate some terms of the relationship. BUT. . . we want to limit the distance. . . or scope. . . or danger.

We say we want to follow where God is leading. BUT. . .

The third piece of "God's Focus"—His protection through anything and everything—we swiftly shy away from. We definitely want God's protection. Trouble is, we don't really want to be in any situation dangerous enough to warrant God's guardian angels having to come to our aid and rescue.

The last thing we want is to be in a position of torture, abuse, whips, chains, dungeons, stonings, being sawed in two, or murdered. Which is really too bad.

By wanting things to be safe and simple, we place limitations on God's creativity. We restrict God's ability to use us in the creative ways that will have the most remarkable impacts on people's lives. By wanting the Holy Spirit to only lead us in safe and boring ways, we forget the greatest aspect of living under "God's Focus"—whatever we attempt in Jesus' name cannot fail!

In Ephesians 2, Paul lets us in on a huge secret—"We are God's workmanship, created in Christ Jesus to do good works, which God prepared in advance for us to do" (Ephesians 2:10, NIV).

Before we were born, God laid out what He wanted us to do. If He has created the works for us, we cannot fail! Whatever we attempt in service to God may not turn out as we envisioned. But we can be certain, whatever comes about from what we attempt is part of the "good works, which God prepared in advance for us to do." Even if what we attempt leads to our own martyrdom, the Triune God will use our death to His glory and for the good of His kingdom.

Under "God's Focus," there is absolutely no excuse for our guardian angels to be bored!

Here, then, is another question—

- What is it you know you are supposed to do?

Small or large—if God is requiring you to do something, excuses and procrastination will never bring God glory!

If you are putting off until tomorrow what God is requiring of you today, you are being disobedient, and you are causing your guardian angel to be bored to tears. . . quite probably, wishing for a transfer to the choir.

If you are not doing what God is requiring of you. . . God, Himself, just might be shedding a tear over your missed faith development.

What is it you know God is requiring of you?

- Forgive someone. . .
- Make a career change. . .
- Trust God with your finances. . .
- Invite someone to worship. . .
- Confess a sin. . .
- Begin a ministry. . .
- Travel to a mission field. . .

"The Prophets: God's Focus"

The reality is "God's Focus" is on you. "God's Focus" is waiting to see how you will respond to what He is leading you to do. And, do not forget—no response is a response in and of itself.

As you think about how you will follow through in the "good works" God is requiring of you, stop reading this book and go for a long walk. As you walk around the neighborhood—

- Pray!
- Pray for God's Spirit to remove any excuses and procrastination from you.
- Pray for God's Spirit to fill you with a willingness to put the "faith of leap"[1] into action.
- Pray for God's Spirit to grant you the trust needed to follow wherever He leads. . . and into whatever He leads you.

Chapter 23

"Us: God's Plan"

After 19 individuals, one group of people ("the prophets"), and three events (creation, the Red Sea, and Jericho's Wall), Hebrews 11 makes this final statement—

> Not one of these people, even though their lives of faith were exemplary, got their hands on what was promised. God had a better plan for us: that their faith and our faith would come together to make one completed whole, their lives of faith not complete apart from ours (Hebrews 11:39-40).

At the pinnacle of everything written about faith and "the Hero of Faithfulness," it is now our turn to take center stage—"God had a better plan for us."

"God's Plan" for us—for YOU!—is that knowing His faithfulness to the men and women in the Bible YOU will grow in your faith, trust, and relationship with Him.

"God's Plan" for us—for YOU!—is that knowing His attributes as displayed in the lives of these men and women YOU will be spurred to action as you live out your faith, trust, and relationship with Him.

What God originally planted in us as a small seed of saving faith, He desires to grow dominant in our heart, soul, mind, strength, and actions.

Matthew 13 contains one parable after another. In the middle of the chapter, Jesus tells "The Parable of the Mustard Seed"—

> The kingdom of heaven is like a mustard seed, which a man took and planted in his field. Though it is the smallest of all your seeds, yet when it grows, it is the largest of garden plants and becomes a tree, so that the birds of the air come and perch in its branches (Matthew 13:31-32, NIV).

If you Google "mustard tree," you will quickly see all kinds of pictures of crazy, wild, out of control plants. Mustard seeds are so small they can be mixed into the most flavorful condiment. Yet the mustard tree grows from one incredibly small seed to an outrageously large, wild, and unkempt tree.

"The Hero of Faithfulness" desires "mustard tree-like" radical growth in our faith. Far from the square-cut, boxed-in, "show-up-most-Sundays," minimal faith most of us live, God desires us to grow large, crazy, wild, and out of control.

"God's Plan"—God's "better plan for us"—is that your faith, when influenced by God's attributes, as displayed in the lives of the men and women of the Bible, will become "one completed whole."

Far too often, however, we live as if we are content being a tiny mustard seed. We live as if we are content with weak, flavorless, nondescript faith. We struggle to believe and live as a mustard tree. We stunt our growth and live as if we have been barely saved by Jesus and only slightly set free from sin.

However, as Ephesians 1 reminds us—

> Because of the sacrifice of the Messiah, His blood poured out on the altar of the Cross, we're a free people—free of penalties and punishments chalked up by all our misdeeds. And not just barely free, either. *Abundantly* free! He thought of everything, provided for everything we could possibly need, letting us in on the plans He took such delight in making. He set it all out before us in Christ, a long-range plan in which everything would be brought together and summed up in Him, everything in deepest heaven, everything on planet earth (Ephesians 1:7-10, italics in the original).

Did you catch that?

"God's Plan" is not that Jesus has barely freed us from sin, death, and the devil to barely squeak our way through life with weak faith. Because of Jesus Christ and by the presence and power of the Holy Spirit, "God's Plan" is that we are "abundantly free."

This divinely bestowed freedom leads us to grow in faith like a mustard tree. This Holy Spirit granted freedom causes us to grow large and mighty like the mustard tree. This abundant freedom gives us the ability to "make one completed whole" as we live out the faith "God's Plan" has planted in us.

Because of "God's Plan," we each have a choice. We can live out our faith as "Tea Bag Christians," or as "Tea Kettle Christians."

A tea bag gets dunked in a mug of hot water, steeps for a bit, and changes the water into a nice tasting cup of tea. At most, that tea bag can influence another cup or two. In short order, the tea bag grows weak and loses its flavor. Soon, the teabag is cast aside because it is useless.

A tea kettle, on the other hand, heats up, boils, roils, whistles. . . and keeps on singing no matter how hot the situation becomes.

Do you want to live as a tea bag (good for a couple cups) or as a tea kettle (making a joyful noise for as long as "the Water of Life" flows through you)?

Here is the thing about living your faith—

- The Christian life is NOT about WHAT you know.
- The Christian life is about WHO you know.
- And, the Christian life is about HOW you live out WHO you know.
- Living the Christian life is NOT complicated.
- Living the Christian life is as simple as loving God. . . loving others. . . and SERVING BOTH!

"God's Plan" is as straightforward as the response Jesus gave to an expert in the Old Testament Law who approached Him one day.

The exchange goes like this—

> "Teacher... what must I do to inherit eternal life?" "What is written in the Law?" [Jesus] replied. "How do you read it?" [The lawyer] answered: "Love the Lord your God with all your heart and with all your soul and with all your strength and with all your mind," and "Love your neighbor as yourself." "You have answered correctly," Jesus replied. "Do this and you will live." (Luke 10:25b-28, NIV)

Not content to leave well enough alone, the self-righteous legal expert pressed on in search of a legal loophole as he posed one more question for Jesus—"And just how would You define 'neighbor?'" (Luke 10:29, NIV).

To this question, Jesus responded with "The Parable of the Good Samaritan"—

> There was once a man traveling from Jerusalem to Jericho. On the way he was attacked by robbers. They took his clothes, beat him up, and went off leaving him half-dead. Luckily, a priest was on his way down the same road, but when he saw him he angled across to the other side. Then a Levite religious man showed up; he also avoided the injured man. A Samaritan traveling the road came on him. When he saw the man's condition, his heart went out to him. He gave him first aid, disinfecting and bandaging his wounds. Then he lifted him onto his donkey, led him to an inn, and made him comfortable. In the morning he took out two silver coins and gave them to the innkeeper, saying, 'Take good care of him. If it costs any more, put it on my bill—I'll pay you on my way back' (Luke 10:30-35).

The punch line to living the Christian life and putting faith into action comes after the lawyer hears this story. Jesus asks him who the neighbor was. The lawyer responds—"'The one who had mercy on him.' Jesus told him, 'Go and do likewise'" (Luke 10:37, NIV).

Jesus told the lawyer and He says to us—"Go and do the same!"

Put your faith into action by being merciful to those in need of mercy!

Put your faith into action by doing justice for those in need of justice!

Put your faith into action by serving those in need of service!

Along the way, your neighborliness will not only care for the wounded near you, your service just might help the "road to Jericho" be improved for everyone who travels it!

One Friday last summer, as Wendy and I were picking our son, Zane, up from a week at a Christian Camp in the mountains nearby, I had an "A-ha!" moment. The Camp's theme for the summer was—"Heart Fx." The theme was drawn from Deuteronomy 6:5—"Love the Lord your God with all your heart and with all your soul and with all your strength" (Deuteronomy 6:5, NIV).

As we were enjoying the closing worship, I was listening to the kids' testimonies about their great week at camp. At one point, the campers sang a song based on the theme verse. As with all good camp songs, there were hand motions.

When they sang the verse about loving God with all your heart, the motion was to cross your arms over your heart.

To love God with all your mind, led to pointing a finger at your head and tapping against it your noggin.

In the third verse, the motion accompanying loving God with all your soul was to lift your leg and tap the SOLE of your shoe.

As we sang, my mind and heart were rocked by this insight—

- The SOUL of loving the Lord God is found in the actions of our SOLES!
- The actions of our SOLES deepen the love of our SOUL!

Jesus' command—"Go and do likewise"—means we have to put the heart knowledge and head knowledge we have about God and Jesus and grace and forgiveness and love and all things spiritual into action as the SOLES of our feet lead us to serve our neighbors in need.

Really, that is the essence of "God's Plan." If we know "The Hero of Faithfulness" with our minds, we will put our SOLES into action on His behalf. If we love "The Hero of Faithfulness" with our hearts, our SOLES will serve others as He first served us.

"Us: God's Plan"

In a way, there are three progressive steps to putting the SOLES of our relationship with Jesus into action. These three steps are detailed in Luke 5.

One day, Jesus was teaching at the Sea of Galilee. There were so many people crowded around that Jesus was almost pushed off the beach and into the water. To keep from getting His robes wet, Jesus got into a boat beached nearby. Jesus looked at the boat's owner, Simon (later renamed by Jesus as Peter), and asked him to put out a little way into the water.

This first step of a relationship with Jesus is pretty simple. All it really requires is paying attention and listening.

As he cleaned his fish nets, Peter was both paying attention and listening. When Jesus asked, Peter put the boat out into the water so Jesus could teach the people.

Are you paying attention and listening for the opportunities to act that Jesus is laying before you?

The second step of "God's Plan" for an ever-increasing relationship with Jesus requires a little more effort and energy. After Jesus was done teaching, He asked Simon Peter to put the boat out into the deep water for an afternoon of fishing.

This second step requires a little more trust because the request from Jesus is going to be a bit irrational.

Peter was a professional fisherman. Jesus was a carpenter and an itinerant preacher. Peter had worked all night—the best time to catch fish—and had completely struck out. They caught nothing. The fish were not biting. And, now? Peter was told to go fishing in the heat of the day? Even a rank amateur should know that is the worst time to go fishing. Peter was tired and cranky (imagine that!). But he was obedient. He put the boat out into the deep water and let down the nets.

When Jesus asks you to do something slightly irrational (talk to your waitress). . . or somewhat challenging (volunteer at the soup kitchen). . . or seemingly scary (quit your job). . . or possibly even dangerous (go to the foreign mission field)—will you be obedient?

Will you trust Jesus enough to let your nets down into the deep water?

In Peter's case, he received a blessing so great he almost swamped his boat. Such a great number of fish were caught that Peter and his partners' nets began to break. Two boats were almost sunk from the bounteous catch!

Frequently, the blessing received from following faithfully is also a hairs-breadth away from disaster! But don't forget—God is in control!

Your blessing from faithful obedience to Jesus' leadership will overwhelm you. The blessing may or may not be financial. The blessing may or may not be health-related. The blessing you receive from trusting and obediently serving God will ALWAYS BE increased faith—

> When Simon Peter saw this, he fell at Jesus' knees and said, 'Go away from me, Lord; I am a sinful man!' For he and all his companions were astonished at the catch of fish they had taken, and so were James and John, the sons of Zebedee, Simon's partners. (Luke 5:8-10a, NIV)

There is no greater reward than realizing your own weakness and God's incomparable strength.

There is no greater blessing than to be obedient to God's call and to then be astonished at what He accomplishes through your service.

This leads to the third step in the living out of our Christian faith in "God's Plan."

Luke 5:10-11 say—"Then Jesus said to Simon, 'Don't be afraid; from now on you will catch men.' So they pulled their boats up on shore, left everything and followed Him" (Luke 5:10b-11, NIV).

The third piece is to follow and live in submission to Jesus as the ultimate authority of life and over death. This part of "God's Plan" revolves around these two questions—

- Will you be Jesus' disciple?
- Who is Lord of your life?

"God's Plan" for us is that the witness of all the men, women, and events in Hebrews 11 will "come together to make one completed whole, their lives of faith not complete apart from ours" (Hebrews 11:40).

The classic hymn "It Is Well With My Soul" contains this verse—
And, Lord, haste the day when my faith shall be sight,

The clouds be rolled back as a scroll;
The trump shall resound, and the Lord shall descend,
Even so, it is well with my soul.[1]

The refrain of the hymn says—
It is well with my soul,
It is well, it is well with my soul.

Pray about and consider the questions—

- Will you be Jesus' disciple?
- Who is Lord of your life?

When you live "God's Plan" for you, everything truly will be well with your soul.
And... for that matter... everything will be well with your SOLES!

Conclusion

"God: The Hero of Faithfulness!"

The person-by-person, event-by-event walk through Hebrews 11 has shown God's attributes at work then, in the lives of His Old Testament people, and now, in our lives.

The great questions Hebrews 11 lay before us are—

- Will we increase our reliance on God?
- And, if so, will that increased reliance on God see us leap into actions of service to God and others?

By God's grace, the answers to these two questions are simple—YES! The way to implementing the YES of increased reliance on God and greater action for God is not as hard as you might think. After all, we are talking about relying on "The Hero of Faithfulness." From Adam to Jeremiah, we have seen God's faithfulness carry great men and women of the past through anything and everything the world could throw at them.

The same "Hero of Faithfulness" is leading you!

Neither home, nor job—not even family—can cause God's faithfulness to you to wane. Even on those days when God seems distant, you can go to bed, fall fast asleep, and get up the next morning confident. After all—"Because of the Lord's great love we are not consumed, for His compassions never fail. They are new every morning; great is Your faithfulness" (Lamentations 3:22-23, NIV).

As you think about how God is calling you to exercise your faith by leaping into action, come with me to the little town of Cana, in Galilee. This is the site of Jesus' first miracle.

When the wine at a wedding feast began to run out, things got tense. We aren't talking about the last call after a couple hours down at the local VFW Hall, with a no-host bar and a rented chocolate fountain. At Jesus' time, a wedding was a weeklong festival for the entire village and anyone else who showed up.

Make sure to not gloss over the action too quickly. Make sure you get into the essence of the action.

Don't forget these huge details—

- Mary had raised Jesus from birth.
- Mary had seen Jesus through adolescence and into adulthood.
- Now, as Jesus entered His 30s, Mary knew the prophecies she had been pondering in her heart about Him for three full decades were about to be fulfilled.

When Mary, Jesus' mother, learned about the impending shortage of Manischewitz, she went to Jesus. As the flow of wine ebbed, Mary said to Jesus—"Son, they are almost out of wine" (John 2:3).

Read the next words and try to guess Jesus' tone of voice—"Is that any of our business, Mother—yours or Mine? This isn't My time. Don't push Me" (John 2:4).

Cavalier? Rude? Heartless? Honest?

Whatever the inflection of Jesus' words, the important thing is what Mary did with what He said. Perhaps the real miracle at Cana is not so much the water into wine we know comes in a few verses. Maybe the mightiest miracle is found in what Mary does after Jesus puts her off.

Miraculously, Mary remained undeterred. She had faith. . . and she put her faith into action! Mary knew Jesus was the answer to this impending Mogen David fiasco.

Mary left Jesus sitting by the dance floor so she could find the head vintner. When she found him, Mary pointed across the room to Jesus and she said to the sommelier—"Whatever He tells you, do it" (John 2:5).

"God: The Hero of Faithfulness!"

Those six words might be the real miracle at Cana!

Those six words are definitely the key to increased reliance on God's faithfulness—

- "Whatever He tells you, do it."

Mary's simple statement tucked away in John 2 is the way to a life of action and service to others in Jesus' name—

- "Whatever He tells you, do it."

Sure enough, in the time it took to fill six stone jugs with 150 or so gallons of water—talk about a party!—the best wine anyone had ever tasted was created.

"This act in Cana of Galilee was the first sign Jesus gave, the first glimpse of His glory. And His disciples believed in Him" (John 2:11).

After reading all these pages about "The Hero of Faithfulness" and His attributes, let me make sure you hear these next three sentences clearly—

- Jesus is ready and waiting to faithfully give His next sign to you!
- Jesus wants to put the next glimpse of His glory on display in and through you!
- Jesus wants to do greater miracles than turn water into wine, than even to raise the dead, in, with, and through—YOU!

Do you believe this?

Are you ready to let Him?

One of my pet peeves is the way the chapter and verse breaks have been put into the Bible. Scripture was inspired by the Holy Spirit and written by the authors without chapters or verses. They wrote as the Holy Spirit carried them—nouns, verbs, punctuation. But no little numbers superscripted along the way. Chapters and verses were added by monks and copyists sometime between the 4th and 15th centuries.

While I am usually glad for the way these numerical notations help us learn and memorize God's Word. I get peeved when we let the chapters falsely bring division to the flow and thought and idea the Holy Spirit originally inspired.

One awful example of this disruption is at the end of what we call Hebrews 11 and the beginning of Hebrews 12.

Hebrews 12:1-3 are the exclamation point on all "The Hero of Faithfulness" talk we have pondered and pored over in Hebrews 11.

In *The Message*, Hebrews 12:1-3 says—

Do you see what this means—all these pioneers who blazed the way, all these veterans cheering us on? It means we'd better get on with it. Strip down, start running—and never quit! No extra spiritual fat, no parasitic sins. Keep your eyes on *Jesus*, who both began and finished this race we're in. Study how He did it. Because He never lost sight of where He was headed—that exhilarating finish in and with God—He could put up with anything along the way: Cross, shame, whatever. And now He's *there*, in the place of honor, right alongside God. When you find yourselves flagging in your faith, go over that story again, item by item, that long litany of hostility He plowed through. *That* will shoot adrenaline into your souls! (Hebrews 12:1-3, italics in original).

These words at the beginning of Hebrews 12 illuminate the purpose for the entire litany of Hebrews 11—

- "Whatever He tells you, do it!"

The NIV renders Hebrews 12:2 this way—"Let us fix our eyes on Jesus, the author and perfecter of our faith, who for the joy set before Him endured the cross, scorning its shame, and sat down at the right hand of the throne of God" (Hebrews 12:2, NIV).

The essence of fixing our eyes on Jesus is to "look away unto. . ."

We are to look away from ourselves. We are to look away from our lives and troubles. We are to stop looking at anything and everything—good or bad—that entangles us or distracts us from God's faithfulness.

And, we are to look away unto—Jesus. We are to look away toward—Jesus.

Jesus has authored our faith. He has perfected us through His death and resurrection. Look away unto Jesus—His cross, His shame, His resurrection, His grace, His faithfulness.

Why?

Because we will struggle. Not IF we will struggle, but WE WILL struggle. The question is WHEN and HOW we will struggle.

Know this—we will face hardships. We will endure difficulties. We will be tempted to give up and return to the safety of the status quo.

Know this as well—when we face these issues, God is faithful!

Shift back from the NIV to *The Message's* rendering of Hebrews 12:3—"When you find yourselves flagging in your faith, go over that story again, item by item, that long litany of hostility He plowed through. *That* will shoot adrenaline into your souls!" (Hebrews 12:3, italics in original).

Whenever you find yourself flagging in your reliance on God—go over the litany of God's faithfulness again. . . and, then, again. . . and, then, do it again. . . and. . .

When you find yourself inactive and not serving—"Look away unto" the examples of "The Hero of Faithfulness." Let God's great faithfulness "shoot adrenaline into your souls!"

As you feel that Holy Spirit infused rush of adrenaline in your soul, let the SOLES of your feet get back into service and action!

Mark Twain famously said—"Twenty years from now you will be more disappointed by the things that you didn't do than by the ones you did do. So throw off the bowlines. Sail away from the safe harbor. Catch the trade winds in your sails. Explore. Dream. Discover."[1]

Don't look back in twenty years and wonder—

- What if I had listened to God. . .
- What if I had acted on my faith. . .

Don't look back tonight and think—

- I should have. . .
- If only. . .

Resolve—by the power of the Holy Spirit—to leave your sail away from the safe harbor!

Resolve—by the power of the Holy Spirit—to test the extremes of God's faithfulness!

Resolve—by the power of the Holy Spirit—to catch the trade winds in your sail and put Mary the Mother of Jesus' instructions into action—

- "Whatever He tells you, do it!"

Endnotes

Introduction- "God: The Hero of Faithfulness"

1. Steven Curtis Chapman, "Faithful," *Beauty Will Rise*, 2009, Sparrow Records.
2. Thomas Edison, http://www.brainyquote.com/quotes/quotes/t/thomasaed132683.html, accessed 3/28/12.

Chapter 1- "Creation: God's Nature"

1. James Cameron, http://www.csmonitor.com/Science/2012/03 27/What-James-Cameron-saw-6.8-miles-deep-in-Mariana-Trench-video, accessed 4/1/12.

Chapter 5- "Abram: God's Call"

1. Oswald Chambers, http://utmost.org/classic/called-of-god-classic/, accessed 4/15/12.
2. Ibid., italics in the original.
3. Ibid.
4. http://info.mapquest.com/terms-of-use/, accessed 4/15/12.

Chapter 6- "Sarah: God's Joy"

1. http://www.allenklein.com/articles/laughterhumormyth.htm, accessed 12/19/12.

2. For a complete discussion on becoming more and more thankful for God's presence and blessings in your everyday life, read *Radical Gratitude: Discovering Joy through Everyday Thankfulness*, by Ellen Vaughn and Charles Colson, Zondervan, 2005. Also, Mark Batterson has great insight into the collecting of "spiritual mementos" (aka: *ebenezers*). Search the archives at: www.markbatterson.com for blogs posts and references in his writings.

Interlude- "God's Sovereignty"

1. Jonas, Robert A., excerpt from *Henri Nouwen*, http://www.spiritualityandpractice.com/books/excerpts.php?id=17109, accessed 4/25/12.
2. Ibid.

Chapter 7- "Abraham & Isaac: God's Intervention"

1. http://www.aetv.com/intervention/about/, accessed 5/8/12.
2. Ibid.
3. Amy Grant, "Angels," *Straight Ahead*, 2007, Amy Grant Productions under exclusive license to Sparrow Records.

Chapter 8- "Isaac: God's Heritage"

1. Leonard Sweet, *I Am A Follower*, Thomas Nelson, 2012, p. 167.
2. Arthur G. Bennett, ed., *Valley of Vision: A Collection of Puritan Prayers and Devotions*, Banner of Truth, 1975, p. 8.

Chapter 9- "Jacob: God's Blessings"

1. Garrison Keillor, http://www.brainyquote.com/quotes/quotes/g/garrisonke137097.html, accessed 8/3/12.
2. Garrison Keillor, http://www.brainyquote.com/quotes/quotes/g/garrisonke106453.html, accessed 8/3/12.

Chapter 10- "Joseph: God's Dreams"

1. Steven Curtis Chapman, "Do Everything," *Re-creation*, 2011, Sparrow Records.

Chapter 11- "Moses' Parents: God's Beauty"

1. Mike Warnke, *Alive!*, 1976, Myrrh Records.

Chapter 13- "Israel & The Red Sea: God's Glory"

1. This quote is attributed far and wide. Most frequently, credit is given to Thomas Merton, although no definitive location in his writings can be found. Recently, Jobonanno and the Godsons released a song by this title on their album *Can't Stop Now*, 2009, Sharkskin Records.

Chapter 14- "Israel & Jericho: God's Posture"

1. Patrick Lencioni, "In-Between Time," *Pat's POV*, July 2012, The Table Group Inc.
2. I was introduced to the concept of waiting, wondering, and praying for your "Jericho," by Mark Batterson, in *The Circle Maker: Praying Circles Around Your Biggest Dreams and Greatest Fears*, 2012, Zondervan.

Chapter 15- "Rahab: God's Inclusivity"

1. Images of Van Gogh's painting "The Church at Auvers" are easily viewable by googling "Van Gogh Church at Auvers," or you can go to http://www.vangoghgallery.com/catalog/Painting/62/Church-at-Auvers,-The.html, accessed 1/24/13.
2. Casting Crowns, "Does Anybody Hear Her?", *Lifesong*, 2005, Reunion Records.

Interlude- "God's Sovereignty... Continues"

1. http://www.historymakers.info/inspirational-christians/gladys-aylward.html, accessed 9/29/12.

Chapter 16- "Gideon: God's Vulnerability"

1. Sweet, p. 166.
2. Ibid., p. 106.

Chapter 18- "Samson: God's Strength"

1. Skye Jethani, *With: Reimagining the Way You Relate to God*, 2011, Thomas Nelson, p.61, italics in original.

Chapter 19- "Jephthah: God's Promise"

1. Thin Lizzy, "The Boys Are Back In Town," *The Definitive Collection*, 2006, Universal Music Enterprises, a Division of UMG Recordings, Inc.

Chapter 20- "David: God's Heart"

1. Blaise Pascal, http://thinkexist.com/quotation/there_is_a_god_shaped_vacuum_in_the_heart_of/166425.html accessed 10/18/12.

Chapter 21- "Samuel: God's Ear"

1. John Zumwalt, teaching "Perspectives," at Calvary Bible Church, Hailey, ID, 8/28/12.

Chapter 22- "The Prophets: God's Focus"

1. For a thorough discussion of "the faith of leap," as opposed to the more frequently talked about "leap of faith," see Michael

Frost and Alan Hirsch, *The Faith of Leap: Embracing a Theology of Risk, Adventure and Courage*, 2011, Baker Books.

Chapter 23- "Us: God's Plan"

1. Horatio G. Spafford, "It Is Well With My Soul," 1873, public domain.

Conclusion- "God: The HERO of Faithfulness!"

1. Mark Twain, http://thinkexist.com/quotation/twenty_years_from_now_you_will_be_more/215220.html, accessed 10/29/12.

Acknowledgements

I have always been drawn to words. Finally getting to string 70,000 or so together into this book has been a dream come true!

Significant to the creation of this volume has been the support of friends almost too numerous to count...

April, your prayers, time, and insights reading the first draft were beyond value! Susan and Chandy, I am grateful for your reading and help, as well. Grandma Judy, Grandma Marge, and others who sampled all or parts of this effort—thank you! Ted, you were one of my earliest cheerleaders. Jon Wiese, your emails of support were divinely timed! Bob, when I hurt my knee and couldn't paint for you any longer, not only were you glad you didn't have to fix any more of my bad caulk jobs, you gave me the most needed advice—make writing my 9-5 job.

Most of my writing was done in "offices" around Hailey. Gallons of Safari Sunset Tea were consumed while writing drafts of these pages at Hailey Coffee Company. Likewise, the ladies of the Hailey Public Library always had a smile and kind word for me as I spread out on the back table!

On just about every page, there are echoes from my English teachers at Pilgrim Lutheran School, Westbury High School, and Concordia College. Especially clear is the voice of my Senior English teacher at Westbury High School, Mrs. Reed. With a wrinkled nose from the stench of my work, she would hand back my essays dripping with red ink, mostly saying "Pronoun Reference Error." Thank you, Mrs. Reed, for teaching me the value of nouns and names—and the proper place for pronouns!

2012 was a year of great transition for me. I left parish ministry after 20 years and finally began to pursue the life of a writer. From the midst of the journey to write this book, I paid some of the bills by working numerous different jobs: teacher at Kinderwelt Preschool, groundskeeper for the Blaine County Recreation District baseball and softball fields, umpire of baseball and softball games, Camp Cook at Camp Perkins Lutheran Outdoor Ministries, window washer for Sun Valley Window Cleaning, soccer and basketball referee, and painter. In many and various ways, each of these jobs helped me see God's faithfulness in greater fullness. Every time I began to wonder if I should write or "get a real job," God brilliantly (and sometimes, painfully) made His desires clear.

Because of all the transitions I put my family through, I cannot begin to express the fullness of my gratitude to them! Leaving behind two decades of parish ministry to begin an unknown adventure, in the middle of a troubled economy, requires the support and commitment of special people. My wife and kids have shown me that commitment and support. . . and then some! They have also extended me grace beyond grace as the adventure of the past year has unfolded!

> Wendy—you are the embodiment of a "help-meet! You are the best wife a man could pray for! You are also the greatest mother to our children!
>
> Zane—thank you for coming home from school most days and asking if I wrote anything that day. You kept me honest and on track!
>
> Mallory—your smile and laugh inspire me. . . even if your energy wears me out! God knew what He was doing when He led us to make "Joy" your middle name!
>
> One last word. . .

To everyone who has a dream that has been sitting on the back burner of your imagination for long enough, this book is living proof that God really is "The Hero of Faithfulness!" He really is able to accomplish "immeasurably more than all we ask or imagine!"

Acknowledgements

Don't wake up in 20 years despondent that you didn't follow where God was leading! Make today the day you begin to draw on the example of "The Hero of Faithfulness" to the men and women in Hebrews 11! The only way to know where "The Hero of Faithfulness" will lead you is to take the first step of following Him!

As you live out your God-sized dream, make Paul's doxology in Ephesians 3 the battle cry of your leap into the greatest adventure you will ever enjoy—

"Now to Him who is able to do immeasurably more than all we ask or imagine, according to His power that is at work within us, to Him be glory in the church and in Christ Jesus throughout all generations, for ever and ever! Amen" (Ephesians 3:20-21, NIV).

Steve Barckholtz
Hailey, Idaho
1/31/13

CPSIA information can be obtained at www.ICGtesting.com
Printed in the USA
BVOW031240080413

317591BV00002B/3/P